EARLY GAINSBOROUGH:

'From the obscurity of a Country Town'

Mark Bills and Rica Jones

Published by Gainsborough's House Society, Sudbury, Suffolk, United Kingdom.

Editor: Joyce H. Townsend
Production: Liz Cooper
Designed by Steve Hayes
Printed by Lamport Gilbert

© Gainsborough's House Society and authors

ISBN: 978-0-946511-64-8

With very grateful thanks to John Osborn

Cover: Thomas Gainsborough (1727-1788),
Mr & Mrs John Browne and their daughter, Anna Maria, c. 1754-55
Oil on canvas, 80 x 104 cm.
© Private Collection Norfolk UK

CONTENTS

PREFACE

Sir Peter Luff

My real introduction to the work of Thomas Gainsborough was by a university friend, the late Stephen Jones. It was in 1979 when I first visited Gainsborough's House and Stephen was curator. His enthusiasm for the place was infectious and I am sure he would have been delighted by what is happening here, and by this new book on Gainsborough.

The pages that follow bring to light much new research on Gainsborough's early art and life, including the tragedy of a double murder and the impact of the long shadow of debt on the Gainsborough family. What emerges is an artist with a strong and determined vision, someone who remained steadfast in his desire to become a professional painter. Despite his modest upbringing he fulfilled this ambition triumphantly as he created his own distinct and powerful voice and became one of our best-loved artists.

Earlier this year, thanks to National Lottery players, the Heritage Lottery Fund made a grant of £4.5 million to Gainsborough's House for a project to transform the artist's childhood home into a national centre for Gainsborough and to provide a fuller context for the artist's life and art.

This volume is an important part of this process, further establishing the House as a centre for research and understanding of Gainsborough, and making both house and artist accessible to all. With its many new insights into his early life, it is published to coincide with one of the last exhibitions at Gainsborough's House before it is radically expanded to reach a whole new audience. My hope is that both house and book will inspire visitors just as I was inspired forty years ago.

Sir Peter Luff, Chair, Heritage Lottery Fund

ACKNOWLEDGEMENTS

Mark Bills - Director

This book emerges out of several years of research and like all such publications it could only happen with the support of so many.

For a growing institution and with limited resources, we are enormously grateful to those who give us financial support and encouragement. Very special thanks go to John Osborn, whose patronage of this book has meant that we can publish this new research. Grateful thanks go in great measure to the Royal Academy, Art Fund and The Paul Mellon Centre for Studies in British Art. These institutions who do so much to support British art supported research and exhibition of this material.

The staff of Gainsborough's House need to be thanked and particularly Liz Cooper who has done so much work on the far from straightforward production of this book. Thanks also go to Dr Joyce Townsend, Neville Rolt, Steve Hayes and Stephanie Dennison. I am personally grateful to my family for bearing with me, for inevitably research and writing takes place at weekends and holidays.

Particular thanks go to Rica Jones for her contributions, her advice, her research and her conservation of Gainsborough paintings. They also go to Martin Bailey of *The Art Newspaper* for his brilliant discovery in the nick of time, Professor Mark Hallett, Christoph Vogtherr, David Tyler, Alexander Antrim, Karen Hearn, Hugh Belsey, Sue Sloman, Lord Rothschild, Fiona Atkins, Juliet Carey, Naomi Richards, Polly Saltmarsh and owners of Gainsborough's works who cannot be named. The book coincides with the *Early Gainsborough* exhibition at Gainsborough's House and it is a good opportunity to thank the Marquess of Cholmondoley, Philip Mould, the Foundling Museum, private owners, Lowell Libson and Jonny Yarker who have generously loaned to the exhibition.

It is pleasing that the book is so full of images and my thanks go to The British Library, The National Gallery, British Museum, The Whitworth, The University of Manchester, National Gallery of Ireland, National Portrait Gallery, Staatliche Museen zu Berlin, Tate, and The Morgan Library & Museum. A number of institutions gave their images at no cost and my particular thanks go to Houghton Hall, Ipswich Museum Services, James Brocklebank, Douai, Musee de la Chartreuse, Royal Collection at Windsor, The Foundling Museum and the Saint Louis Museum of Art, Missouri.

It is timely that the book is being published at a time where there is great interest in the artist with exhibitions *Early Gainsborough* at Gainsborough's House, *Gainsborough and the Theatre* at the Holburne Museum and *Gainsborough's Family Album* at National Portrait Gallery. I would like to thank all our colleagues in the other institutions for their support and for their passion for Thomas Gainsborough.

Mark Bills, Director of Gainsborough's House

Mark Bills

(Detail of)
Thomas Gainsborough
(1727-1788), *Mr & Mrs John Browne and their daughter, Anna Maria,* c. 1754-55,
Oil on canvas,
80 x 104 cm
© Private Collection
Norfolk UK

When Thomas Gainsborough died on Saturday morning, 2 August at 2 o'clock, very little had been published about his early life. His death heralded an interest in his roots, which found expression in a number of short accounts. Gainsborough had written: 'We love a genius for what he leaves and we mourn him for what he takes away'.[1] With his own death, commentators showed an appetite for revealing what he had taken away, his whole story with its beginning, middle and end. His obituaries re-created a sketchy, but complete life from his birth in Sudbury to his death in Pall Mall. A hastily created biography by Philip Thicknesse and a mixture of anecdotes quickly followed these.[2] Added to this, a small amount of his conversations with his friends and associates have spasmodically appeared in print through memoirs and reminiscences over the decades. Although we are enormously lucky with the number of Gainsborough's letters that survive, very few contain references to his formative years.

With a new century and into the next century too, many books on Gainsborough followed although few were specifically biographical. In the mid-nineteenth century Sudbury's poet and historian George Williams Fulcher (1795–1855) produced an important biography, *The Life of Thomas Gainsborough, R.A.,* where familiarity and tradition serve to fill the gaps, giving us the most detailed, if not always the most accurate, account of Gainsborough's early life.[3] The art historian William Thomas Whitley (1858–1942) did much to redress this with his well-researched biography of the artist, which appeared in 1915.[4]

The scarcity of early sources on the young Gainsborough has meant that the same brief texts have appeared and re-appeared in different incarnations, supplemented with varying degrees of contextual information. If they have failed to answer all the questions they have raised, they have succeeded in moulding our image of the young artist. This idea of the artist has not always been convincing and the temptation has always been to

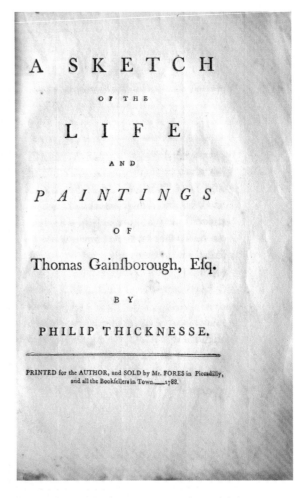

Philip Thicknesse (1719–92) Frontispiece, *A Sketch of the Life and Paintings of Thomas Gainsborough Esq*, [London] Printed for the Author, and Sold by Mr. Fores, 1788
© Gainsborough's House, Sudbury, Suffolk

depict the great oak rather than the acorn, blinded by the great artist Gainsborough became.

When around 1740, Gainsborough, 'quitted Sudbury in his 13th year,'[5] not only was he unknown, but he had to find a living that would bring a regular income. The idea of being a painter, if indeed he had one at that stage, was an ambitious one and required more capital than he had been left by his uncle, Thomas Gainsborough. It is little surprise that there are no written accounts contemporaneous with this period and that the earliest sources were published in August 1788, following Gainsborough's

Thomas Gainsborough
(1727-1788),
Self-Portrait, 1754, Oil
on canvas, 54 x 48cm
© Private Collection
Norfolk UK

death. These three short biographies appeared in that month and were written in turn by Sir Henry Bate Dudley (1745–1824), an unknown friend of Gainsborough, and Philip Thicknesse (1719–1792). The numerous other accounts that appear in the months following are a mixture of all three and, as Whitley commented: 'It is curious that the Ipswich and Bath newspapers published no notes of their own on Gainsborough's death, but were content to reproduce a few paragraphs from London journals'.[6]

This book is in two sections. The first looks again at the surviving accounts and brings forward new ones to give a context for the early life of Thomas Gainsborough. The second section looks at what we can glean from the material evidence of the fabric of the paintings he made earlier in his life and focuses upon Gainsborough's early practice as an artist. Two appendices reproduce in full the obituaries that appeared shortly after Gainsborough's death in August 1788 and the death threats received by Gainsborough's family in 1738.

As Gainsborough's House embarks in 2018 upon a major expansion, it is fitting that the early life of Gainsborough should be explored again, drawing together existing research and publishing for the first time new discoveries at this important time in the artist's life. Beginning with his birth in the historic market town of Sudbury, it follows his move to London, his marriage and return to Sudbury in his early twenties. Within this period Gainsborough learned to be an artist. Even at a young age Gainsborough was an extremely accomplished landscape painter, and his roundel of *Charterhouse* for the Foundling Hospital for example, seems all the more advanced when compared to the other depictions by an older generation of painters that surround it. His developments as a portraitist took a little longer, but by the time he moved to Ipswich in 1752, he had painted some of the greatest 'conversation pieces' of the age. The story of early Gainsborough is the story of how a burgeoning and enthusiastic boy became one of the greatest artists of any age.

Mark Bills

---

[1] Thomas Gainsborough to Henry Bate Dudley 20 June 1787, in John Hayes, *The Letters of Thomas Gainsborough*, London, 2001, No.101.
[2] Philip Thicknesse, *A Sketch of the Life of and Paintings of Thomas Gainsborough, Esq.* London 1788, and accounts (often repeated) in newspapers countrywide.
[3] Fulcher did not complete his biography of Thomas Gainsborough in his lifetime, but it was completed by his son Edmund Syer Fulcher (b.1833) and published in London in 1856. Its popularity ensured that it reached a second edition in the same year.
[4] William T. Whitley, *Thomas Gainsborough*, London, 1915. His extensive notes and clippings for this biography are still an important source for researchers and are held in the British Museum.
[5] Sir Henry Bate Dudley, *Morning Herald*, 4 August 1788.
[6] Whitley, 1915, p308.

'FROM THE OBSCURITY OF A COUNTRY TOWN'

Mark Bills

(Detail of)
The Brewer's Map of Sudbury,
1714, Vellum,
99 x 52 cm
© Sudbury Town
Council, Suffolk
Now Gainsborough's
House, Number 6 was
Alderman Carter's house
in 1714.

EARLY EIGHTEENTH-CENTURY SUDBURY

For Sudbury, the eighteenth century represented a great time of change. During the reign of Queen Anne in 1705, an act of Parliament was passed making the River Stour navigable from Sudbury, Suffolk, to Manningtree, Essex. This was one of the country's earliest statutory rights of navigation. Between 1705 and 1713, work was undertaken to enable passage for barges, boats, lighters and other vessels to the sea. This gave far more trading opportunities that had been previously possible and the town expanded and modernised, which saw many of the older timber-framed properties given a new more regular brick or stucco façade. Gainsborough's House was a good example of a late medieval house, georgianised by the artist's father in the early 1720s. Two most interesting contemporary accounts give a good setting for Gainsborough's birth and time in Sudbury.

The first is a map created by Brewer in 1714, right at the beginning of the Georgian era. It is the first visual image we have of Sudbury and the house that Gainsborough was born in and knew as his family home. It is listed as Alderman Carter's House (No.6 ref no. on the map) on the corner of Curds Lane and Sepulchre Street. The key to the map highlights both landmarks and the houses of the great and the good. There is no mention of the Gainsborough family nor the group of rising merchant dissenters of which they formed a part.

The second is the account of Daniel Defoe from his 1722 tour of East Anglia, which provides us with outline information about the town as it existed when he visited:

> A little to the left is Sudbury, which stands upon the River Stour, mentioned above – a river which parts the counties of Suffolk and Essex, and which is within these few years made navigable to this town, though the navigation does not, it seems, answer the charge, at least not to advantage.

Gainsborough's House, Sudbury
© Gainsborough's House, Sudbury, Suffolk

Gainsborough's House, Sudbury
© Gainsborough's House, Sudbury, Suffolk

I know nothing for which this town is remarkable, except for being very populous and very poor. They have a great manufacture of says and perpetuanas [a durable wool serge fabric], and multitudes of poor people are employed in working them; but the number of the poor is almost ready to eat up the rich. However, this town sends two members to Parliament, though it is under no form of government particularly to itself other than as a village, the head magistrate whereof is a constable.[1]

In many ways the Sudbury Defoe records is a town, like many others, that changed through the major development of its existing industry, in this case wool and weaving. What he failed to mention is the surrounding landscape, perhaps because at the time much of England was rural, or because such matters were of less interest to the writer. As his friend Philip Thicknesse noted,[2] it is 'from the obscurity of a Country Town' that Gainsborough emerged.

---

[1] Daniel Defoe, *Tour through the Eastern Counties of England*, 1722.

[2] Philip Thicknesse, *A Sketch of the Life and Paintings of Thomas Gainsborough*, London, 1788, p.4.

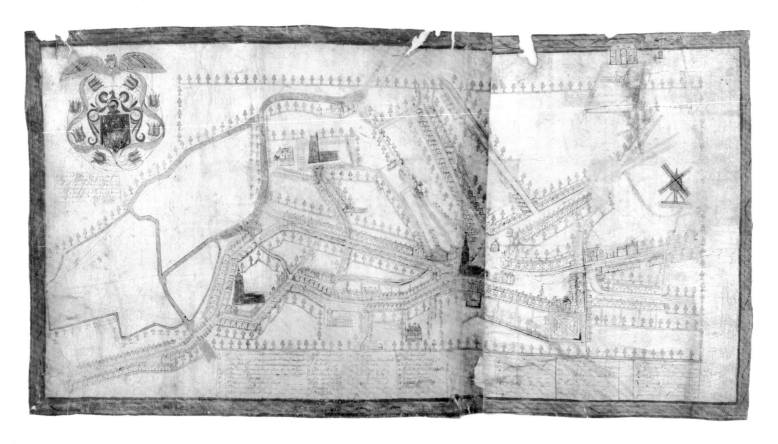

The Brewer's Map of Sudbury, 1714, Vellum, 99 x 52 cm
© Sudbury Town Council, Suffolk

John Theodore Heins
(1697-1756), *Thomas Gainsborough (1709-1738)*, 1731, Oil on canvas, 76.2 x 63.5cm
© Gainsborough's House, Sudbury, Suffolk

THE GAINSBOROUGH FAMILY: 'WITH SOMETHING MYSTERIOUS IN HIS HISTORY'

In one sense Gainsborough's early life was idyllic, a happy childhood that he harked back to throughout his life, seeing it as a bucolic vision of rural life. Sudbury with its surrounding countryside was inspiring to the burgeoning artist, but his life at this time must also have been effected by the turmoil experienced by his family. It has long been recorded that Gainsborough's father faced bankruptcy in 1733, when the artist was six years old. What has not been known is that as well as debt there were often difficult and dangerous business relationships within the more affluent side of the family, who came to the aid of the artist's father and family, the wealthier members being threatened with harm: it appears that two of them were murdered. The impact of this upon the young Gainsborough has not been explored, nor the difficulties he must have experienced with clients who had strained relationships with the Gainsborough family.

Thomas Gainsborough was born in Sudbury in 1727. The exact date of his birth is uncertain, but what we know is that he was baptised at the dissenting chapel on Friars Street on 14 May in 1727, as his name appears in the 'Register of Baptised children belonging to the Congregation of Protestant Dissenters in or about the Town of Sudbury'. 'Thomas the Son of John Gainsborough,' was born into a large family, the youngest of eight surviving children.

His father John Gainsborough had married his mother Mary Burrough on 6 July 1704, a year before her brother Humphrey Burrough entered Corpus Christi College, Cambridge University.[3] This uncle, who went on to take orders in the Church of England was to teach the young Gainsborough at Sudbury Grammar School, where he was Master from 1723 until 1755. Indeed, the most important figures in Gainsborough's early life, apart from his close family, were his two

The Water Meadows, Sudbury
© A.Purkiss

uncles; Humphrey Burrough on his mother's side and Thomas Gainsborough on his father's side, for whom the artist was named. Both were successful in their careers and both were poles apart politically and religiously. Both were the heads of the divided factions that existed in the family.

This is perhaps nowhere better illustrated than at the year of the artist's birth in 1727, which was the year of a general election. Usually the Suffolk Tory candidates were elected unopposed, but in 1727 the two Tory baronets Sir Jermyn Davers and Sir William Barker were opposed when the local Whigs, headed by the Duke of Grafton, the Earl of Bristol, and Lord Cornwallis, put up a candidate named John Holt of Redgrave Hall, Suffolk, who was from a family of merchants and lawyers. The result was unchanged with Davers and Barker returning to their seat, but Holt was close.[4] In the Sudbury section of *A Copy of the Poll for the Knights of the Shire for the County of Suffolk, Taken at Ipswich, Aug 30. Anno Dom. 1727*, the only two members of the family to vote were the two uncles, with the Anglican Reverend Humphry Burroughs voting for the two Tory candidates and Thomas Gainsborow (sic) voting Whig as all the Dissenting merchants did.[5]

In all probability the artist's father John Gainsborough shared the religion and politics of his brother. Most certainly, uncle Thomas was key in shaping the life of the artist and his family through his support and direction. Like his brother there is little doubt that John Gainsborough harboured ambition and it seems, initially at least, that as a businessman he saw some success. He was made a freeman in Sudbury and purchased at least three properties in the town, one of which is now Gainsborough's House. We also know that he renovated and improved the properties including the rather elegant facade of Gainsborough's House. Initial success seems to have petered out

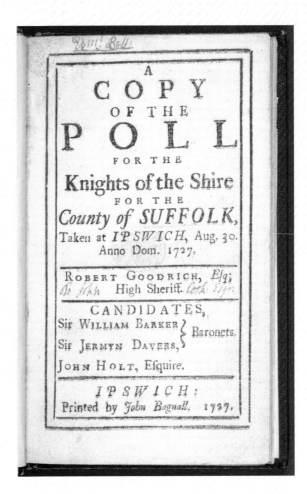

Frontispiece, *A Copy Of the Poll for the Knights of the Shire for the County of Suffolk, Taken at Ipswich, Aug 30. Anno Dom, Ipswich, 1727*, Robert Goodrich, Esq; High Sheriff. Candidates, Sir William Barker, Sir Jermyn Davers, Baronets. John Holt, Esquire © British Library Board, Shelf ref: General Reference Collection 807.b.27.
Frontispiece
An election in the year of Thomas Gainsborough's birth. Two of the artist's family were allowed to vote, both his maternal and paternal uncles.

somewhat. Whether he had overstretched himself or in fact was the victim of addictive pursuits such as drinking or gambling, we shall probably never know.

His financial difficulties came to a head in 1733 when his bankruptcy was announced in June stating that 'John Gainsborough, now or late of Sudbury, in the County of Suffolk, being a Clothier, ... being declared a Bankrupt ...'.[6] In October of the same year the bankruptcy was annulled and it was announced that 'Whereas a commission of Bankrupt was lately awarded against John Gainsborough, of Sudbury, in the County of Suffolk, Clothier, this is to give Notice,

---

[3] 4 July 1710 Humphrey Burrough ordained deacon in London Church of England; 20 December 1713 Rev. Humphrey Burrough becomes a priest in Norwich; 20 December 1717 Humphrey Burrough marries Philippa or Philadelphia Bisbie at St Peters, Sudbury; 1721 Rev Humphrey Burrough becomes Rector of Borley, Essex until his death in 1757; 1723 Rev Humphrey Burrough appointed as Master of Sudbury Grammar School, a role in which he remained until 1755, two years before his death.

[4] Davers 3079, Barker 2963, Havers 2365, from: http://www.historyofparliamentonline.org/volume/1715-1754/constituencies/suffolk - footnote1_k0aphps.

[5] *A Copy of the Poll for the Knights of the Shire for the County of Suffolk, Taken at Ipswich, Aug 30. Anno Dom. 1727. Ipswich 1727.* Sudbury votes are on pp.145–148.

[6] 26 June 1733 in the *London Gazette.*

[7] 16 October 1733 in the *London Gazette.*

[8] Suffolk Record Office E3/32/2.

that the said Commission is superseded under the Great Seal of Great Britain.'[7] It is not clear how this was annulled but one might surmise that it was a mixture of help from his brother, alongside borrowing. We do know that his brother Thomas enabled his own son, John Gainsborough, to buy three Sudbury properties from his financially embarrassed brother, thus allowing the artist's parents to continue to live in their home, albeit as rent-free tenants. It is around this time that the artist's father, having just lost his property, became Postmaster of Sudbury until his death in 1748 when it was taken over by his wife. No doubt strings were pulled so that John Gainsborough could receive a regular and secure income for the rest of his life. The only statement that we have concerning this aspect of his character is within the will of his brother Thomas who stated that 'I am fearfull that should my brother John Gainsborough live many years he may come into such circumstances as may stand in need of some assistance ...'.[8] As a result Thomas made a provision 'that he be paid five shillings a week during his life'

Thomas Gainsborough
(1727-1788), *John Gainsborough* (1683-1748), 1751, Pencil on paper, 9.4 x 7.4 cm
© Gainsborough's House, Sudbury, Suffolk
A posthumous drawing of the artist's father.

rather than any annuity or lump sum, presumably because he realised that a large amount would certainly have been frittered away very quickly. The will certainly had the positive effect of allowing John Gainsborough to avoid poverty as he lived into his early sixties, albeit leaving considerable debts at his death in 1748.

The remaining estate of John Gainsborough was seized by a debtor, Bernard Carter (born 27 November 1713),[9] rather than passing to any of his surviving children: 'Admon of the Goods Chattels and Credits of John Gainsborough, late of Sudbury in the County of Suffolk, deceased, was granted to Bernard Carter a principal creditor of the said deceased'.[10] Carter's father Alderman Bernard Carter had been a previous owner of Gainsborough's House, and his name and property is clearly displayed on the wonderful hand-painted Brewer's map of Sudbury recording the town in 1714. It is perhaps ironic, though probably no coincidence, that it was a branch of that illustrious Sudbury family that Gainsborough painted in *Mr and Mrs Carter*, 1745–6 (Tate) and more famously in one of Gainsborough's most iconic works, *Mr and Mrs Andrews,* c.1750 (National Gallery, London) which depicts Mrs Andrews (*née* Frances Carter), the daughter of William and Frances. Given the rather peculiar depiction of Mr and Mrs Carter, and the unfinished element of *Mr and Mrs Andrews*, with the Gainsboroughs so beholden to the Carters at the time that they were painted, it begs a question as to the nature of the commissions.

In *Mr and Mrs Carter,* we see the portrait of William Carter, looking rather old-fashioned and vulgar in his out-dated wig and flamboyant waistcoat. Compared to the usually restrained colour and elegant form of his painting of couples in this period, such as *(John) Joshua and Sarah Kirby (née Bull)* c.1751–52, (National Portrait Gallery) this is an oddity. The diminutive figure of his wife has pallid features which make her look all the more fragile, and hints at 'long-suffering'. The portrait, which according to a note by John Bensusan-Butt was by family tradition, 'a gift to the sitters in

(Detail of) John Theodore Heins (1697-1756), *Thomas Gainsborough (1709-1738),* 1731, Oil on canvas, 76.2 x 63.5cm
© Gainsborough's House, Sudbury, Suffolk
Gainsborough's cousin and namesake was murdered at the age of 29.

return for favours done to Gainsborough',[11] raises questions as to the nature of those favours. It must have been an uncomfortable painting for Gainsborough to paint and possibly implies that it covered the debt to the family. Certainly this fits with the dating as 1746–7, as William Carter died shortly after Gainsborough's father on 27 November 1748. Given the context of his father's growing debt, one cannot escape seeing an element of Hogarthian satire within the work.

John Gainsborough's complete ruin had been guarded against by his brother Thomas who had succeeded far better in business than his brother and had become a pillar of the community. We are fortunate that in the early 1730s he had been wealthy enough to commission the fashionable painter John Theodore Heins (1697–1756) to paint the family in several paintings, two of which now form part of the collection at Gainsborough's House. This is particularly apt as they are probably some of the first paintings Thomas Gainsborough saw, being in the house of his uncle and cousins in Sudbury.

Thomas was a religious man and his patronage of Sudbury's dissenting chapel is well recorded, including

---

[9] General Record Office J522/16.
[10] General Record Office, PROB 6/124/204.
[11] John Bensusan-Butt, *Thomas Gainsborough in his Twenties*, Colchester, 1993, p.67.
[12] Suffolk Record Office E3/32/2.

John Theodore Heins
(1697-1756), *John
Gainsborough* (1711-1772),
1731, Oil on canvas,
76.2 x 63.5 cm
© Gainsborough's House,
Sudbury, Suffolk
Thomas Gainsborough's
cousin, the purchaser of
Gainsborough's House
following the bankruptcy of
the artist's father in 1733.

in its trust deed of 29 November 1710 when the Friars Street chapel was built, recording Gainsborough's family as one of the biggest donors, and having a family vault and allocated pews. His charitable giving is also recorded and he appears, from the outside at least, to be a paragon of respectability. His religious commitment is also very prominently illustrated by his patronage of Humphrey Gainsborough, the artist's older brother. In his will Thomas expressed this: 'I

have some years past taken upon my self the care of Humphrey Gainsborough and of the son of my brother John Gainsborough who is now in London a pupil at the Academy where Mr Eames is Master in order to be trained up for the Ministry. My will is that my executors do pay twenty pounds a year towards defraying the charges that may attend his being trained up as above said for three years from the Date hereof'.[12] There is little doubt that he approved of

Humphrey's religious calling and encouraged Humphrey to study at the dissenting Moorfields Academy, Tenter Lane, under the Rev. John Eames (1686–1744), a friend of Isaac Newton.

His religious conviction gave him links with similar dissenting Protestants, with business connections both at home and abroad. The Huguenots and the New World also provided further business opportunities. It appears, however, that some of their associations were less than agreeable and there is a certain amount of mystery surrounding their practice. Even the artist's father John Gainsborough was eyed with some suspicion by the residents of Sudbury. In a posthumous drawing by his son (Gainsborough's House, 1751) we see something of the character of John, a man who was, according to Allan Cunningham: 'by trade a clothier, and in religion a dissenter, I can only say with common belief that he was a stately and personable man, with something mysterious in his history, for the pastoral and timid rustics of Suffolk suspected him of carrying a dagger and pistols under his clothes.'[13]

The will of his brother Thomas Gainsborough (1678–1739) provides much of the early evidence we have of the artist and his family. The circumstance leading to Thomas's death in March 1739, particularly the last two years, reveal a very different aspect of the Gainsborough family. Thomas was born in 1678 and had 7 children. His eldest son (1709–38), painted by the German *emigrée* artist Heins in 1731, following tradition was also called Thomas, and was like his father a successful man of business, setting up in London with a partner called Samuel Storke. The business appears to have very lucrative from the sums accounted through various bank entries, and had a close connection with America.

Thomas and his eldest son Thomas came into the path of very dangerous men due to the bankruptcy of an associate John Barnard, a Mercer of Sudbury. Thomas was a major creditor of Barnard's and because of this

and Sudbury being his own town, he was empowered to claim all the debts due to Barnard. One of the debtors was Richard Brock of Margate's Inn. The bankruptcy took place in 1732 and for several years following, Thomas and his son pursued Brock for the payment of his debt, with no positive result. Brock later claimed that he had offered to pay £14 to Thomas Gainsborough junior, which was said later to be untrue by the creditors. Legal action was prosecuted through the Sudbury Attorney Samuel Sabine, resulting on 1 March 1737-8 in a letter sent to Sudbury from London and 'received by the said Thomas Gainsborough, threatening him, his Son, and another Person [Sabine] with Death, unless he immediately complied with certain Conditions therein mentioned.'[14]

The threat accuses uncle Thomas, his son Thomas, and Sabine of effectively ruining Brock's family through the pursuing the debt: 'I understand that you have Runed [ruined] my frind [friend] Brock to all Intents and Purposes, which you must Expect to suffer, for Runen [ruining] a family so Basely as you have done; that is, I mean in the next World you must expect to suffer for, in this I know your Welth [wealth] will proteckt [protect] you' The unknown author of the threat also alludes to the impact on the wider family 'you have Runed [ruined] Brocks Mother, for shee was Bound for 70 Pounds for him, and now the Bayles [bayliffs] have got shee [her], and all thorrough your Roges [rogues] tricks; so Revenge is Sweet.'

The actual threat contained within the letter surrounds various ways in which they might be killed if they do not release Brock from the debt: 'for unless you Release our friend Brock, if you Bring a troop of men with you to aid you, we will have you from him: Their is 10 or 12 of us that know you all 3; we should have had sume of you before now... If you keep from Coming to toun, we will come Doune [down] and blow you up with Gunpowder. God dam you all... if you Don't acquit him Directly, he shall be shure [sure] to give you a Meel [meal] that you will not like.'

[13] Cunningham on John Gainsborough (the painter's father). Allan Cunningham, *The Lives of the Most Eminent British Painters,* revised by Mrs. Charles Heaton, London, 1842, vol.1, p.258.
[14] Threat dated 1 March 1737-8 from the *Daily Gazetteer,* 24 October 1738. With many thanks to Martin Bailey of *The Art Newspaper* for the discovery of the *Daily Gazetteer* article.
[15] Threat dated 3 September 1738 from the *Daily Gazetteer,* 24 October 1738.

The threats also particularly focus upon the young Thomas Gainsborough, the artist's cousin, resident in London threatening that at '…the first Site [sight], we will Either shute [shoot] him [the artist's cousin] or hang him up in Jebbets [Gibbets]; Dam[n] the Roge [rogue], we was within a Little of his Rogges Ass [rogue's arse] not a Week ago.'

The threat was taken very seriously to the point where Thomas made the threat public. We know this through a reference in the second threat that appeared: 'you know you published the former letter; but take care you don't do the like now.'[15]

Importantly, both father and son to make made wills around the time of the threats; Thomas Gainsborough junior on 20 September 1737 at the young age of 28 and

the Thomas Gainsborough senior at the age of 59 some time that same year. It must have been clear to them that there was real danger in the recovery of the debt.

There is no further correspondence for six calendar months. Brock was not relieved of his debt. So a second, even more vehement threat followed. Written on 3 September 1738 it was sent with the same aim in mind, with a specific threat against the artist's cousin: 'Mr. Gainsborough, fail not of Quiting [acquitting] Brock Directly of his Troble [trouble]; if you dont, by G— Revenged of him your Sun[son] we sertainly [certainly] will be. I am your friend, to Acquaint you of the Real design, for as shure [sure] as ever he was born, he will be put to an Onmersisuest [ominous] end…' Most chillingly, the offenders had Gainsborough's

The London Gazette,
Saturday September 30 and Tuesday October 3, 1738
Announcement offering a reward for finding the person responsible for the death threats against the Gainsborough family.

> *Whitehall, Sept. 28, 1738.*
> *Whereas two Anonymous Letters, directed to Mr. Thomas Gainsborough, in Sudbury in Suffolk, one dated London, March 1, 1737, and the other, London, September 3, 1738, were received by the said Thomas Gainsborough, threatning him, his Son, and another Person with Death, unless he immediately complied with certain Conditions therein mentioned : His Majesty, for the better discovering and bringing to Justice the Person or Persons concerned in writing and sending the said Letters, is pleased to promise his most gracious Pardon to any one of them, that shall discover his Accomplice or Accomplices, so as they, or any of them, may be apprehended and convicted thereof.*
> *HOLLES NEWCASTLE.*
> *And as a further Encouragement to such Discovery, I do hereby promise to pay the Sum of Thirty Pounds to any Person or Persons who shall discover his Accomplice or Accomplices, so as he or they be convicted thereof.*
> *John Gainsborough,*
> *of Sudbury in Suffolk.*

Thomas Gainsborough
(1727 - 1788), *Mr and Mrs Carter*, c.1747-8,
Oil on canvas,
912 x 710 mm
Thomas Gainsborough's extraordinary portrait of the Carters, the family to whom the artist's father was in debt to.

cousin in their sights, but laid off attacking him because he was in the presence of his wife: 'Our Company mett [met] him upon the Rode sume [some] time ago with his Wife; but we, for the sake of the pore [poor] Woman forebore;' This time the letter gives a very clear time ultimatum. Written on Wednesday 3rd September it wrote: 'if you dont send to Brocks Wife in a Weeks time, with a free Discharge, our whole Care will be to laye wait for him.' The murderous writer made clear that there would be no mercy the next time after that, 'after the time above is Expired, his Life shall suffer; this is the last Notice that shall Ever be given by Any of our Company;' They also made it clear that were not intimidated by Thomas carrying a pair of pistols for protection: 'tis not his Carring [carrying] his brace [pair] of Pistales [pistols] that shall frighton [frighten] us, or Protect him'.

The ultimatum expired on Wednesday 10 September and on the following Monday, 15 September the artist's cousin was dead and buried in Sudbury at the age of 29. For his body to be brought back to his hometown from London and the funeral arrangements to be made he must have been murdered just after the ominous deadline had passed.

As a result, John Gainsborough of Sudbury (the artist's father) approached the Secretary of State, Thomas Pelham-Holles, 1st Duke of Newcastle in order to be able to offer a pardon to those who would offer evidence that would lead to the capture of the culprits: 'His Majesty, for better discovering and bringing to Justice the Person or Persons concerned in writing and sending the said Letters is pleased to promise his most gracious Pardon to any one of them, that shall discover his Accomplice or Accomplices, so as they, or any of them, may be apprehended and convicted thereof.'[16] To this they added the sum of thirty pounds reward 'as a further Encouragement to such discovery'. It seems inconceivable given the nature of the letters and that they would go to such lengths for any other circumstance than murder. The *London Gazette* published details of the reward on 26 and 30 September 1738 with the *Daily Gazetteer*, publishing the threats themselves on 24 October.

The murder of his son clearly only served to stiffen the resolve of Thomas Gainsborough senior and he continued to sue Brock although the threat did not go away. 'By god you shall never Come to London Safe; for, Dam[n] you, we will have no more Massey [mercy] than the Devil will have of you; and your Roge of a Lawyer shall, certainly drink out of the same Cup[p],' the threat had warned. Exactly six months later when the culprits were still at large Thomas visited London and, it appears, was also murdered. The *Weekly Miscellany*, on 17 March 1739, reported his death that had taken place a week before: ''March 10, *Died...* At the Golden Fleece in Cornhill, Mr. Gainsborough, a Crepe-Factor of Sudbury'. The Golden Fleece, a pub in Cornhill in the City of London, was very near to the coach stop from Sudbury and was used by visitors to the metropolis.

Thomas Gainsborough senior had remade his will on 23 February 1739 and died at the age of 61. He is buried alongside his son in Sudbury. Within six months of the second death threat, both men who had been threatened were dead. Looking at the Heins picture of Thomas Gainsborough junior painted in 1731, the portrait depicts the artist's cousin at the age of 22 at the end of his apprenticeship to James Ball, Merchant Tailor, a young man with the world before him. Three years after the portrait was painted he was partner with Samuel Storke operating as Messrs Storke & Gainsborough in the City of London. Four years later he was murdered.

The murder of Uncle Thomas had a very direct impact upon the young artist. Thomas Gainsborough was favoured by him, and alongside his brother Humphrey, they received the most generous legacies left among John's eight children, their uncle clearly wishing to give them both a good start in life. The opportunity must have been tied up with conflicting feeling united with his sadness for the loss.

---

[16] *London Gazette*, 26 and 30 September 1738.

FIRST STEPS IN DRAWING

Gainsborough's natural instinct for landscape painting is perhaps not so surprising, when one considers that Gainsborough grew up in the rural market town of Sudbury in Suffolk, surrounded by countryside which still evokes his paintings and drawings. Philip Thicknesse, Gainsborough's first biographer, who published his anecdotal sixty-one page booklet within months of the artist's death, recalled: 'that there was not a Picturesque clump of Trees, nor even a single Tree of beauty, no, nor hedgerow, stone, or post, at the corner of the Lanes, for some miles round about the place of his nativity, that he had not so perfectly in his *mind's eye,* that ... he could have perfectly delineated.'[17] Thicknesse was not alone in emphasising the inspiration of nature to Gainsborough. Sir Henry Bate Dudley (1745–1824), one of Gainsborough's great supporters, wrote in his obituary of the artist, 'That nature was his teacher and the woods of Suffolk his academy'.[18] Sir Joshua Reynolds in his eulogistic Academy Discourse which followed Gainsborough's death, noted that his landscapes were 'a portrait-like representation of nature, such as we see in the works of Rubens, Ruysdaal, and others of those schools.'[19]

The idea of Gainsborough as an entirely natural and self-taught artist was prevalent in the late eighteenth century. Yet this is misleading, for even though he was possessed with a great deal of natural talent, training was still necessary. Nature is a mass of fragmented colour, shade and forms, but a painting is a cohesive and harmonious whole. It was only by studying the work of other artists, being trained by them alongside his enthusiastic observation of nature that Gainsborough developed his own sophisticated painterly world.

Later accounts of Gainsborough's early life give an even more romantic view of the developing artist. In the nineteenth century, Fulcher, a Sudbury man, fleshed out all the detail of his early life, whilst reflecting on his natural genius. Fulcher recorded an incident when Gainsborough played truant, returning in the evening, 'his paper filled with woodland scenery ... oaks and elms of majestic growth, clumps of trees and winding glades ...' which 'plainly indicated his love of the art.'[20] This is a captivating but slightly fanciful and much later account of the burgeoning genius. Gainsborough's mother was from an Anglican family, and it is generally thought that she was 'a women of cultivation, and an amateur painter.'[21]

Before Gainsborough went to study in London, where his older brother and members of his family were already resident, he did not go entirely without any training, An important aspect of his early training has been overlooked. This is the influence of a close family friends with strong artistic leanings, who played a pivotal role in Gainsborough's artistic development; the Coyte family. The *Morning Chronicle* wrote that: 'In the neighbourhood of his father was a very respectable clergyman of the name of Coyte; with the sons of this gentlemen young Gainsborough and his brothers passed much of his time, and from the instructions of the old man, reaped some advantage ... the young Coytes lent him their drawing-books; and the boy shewing extreme eagerness in the pursuit, wandering through fields, meadows, and woods, in search of rural scenes, became talked of in the neighbourhood.'[22]

Drawing books were available at this time for drawing the figure, physiognomy, and stance, as well as landscapes. A number of drawing books were published in London in the 1730s which would have

(Detail of)

Thomas Gainsborough (1727 – 1788), 'Self-portrait of the artist sketching' 1754 – 1757, pencil on paper, 359 x 258 mm ©The Trustees of the British Museum

[17] Thicknesse, 1788, p.6.

[18] Sir Henry Bate Dudley, *Morning Herald,* 4 August, 1788.

[19] John Burnet (ed.), *The Discourses of Sir Joshua Reynolds,* London, 1842, p.248.

[20] George William Fulcher, *The Life of Thomas Gainsborough, R.A.* This work was completed by Fulcher's son Edmund Syer Fulcher (b.1833) and published in London in 1856, see p.25.

[21] William T. Whitley, *Thomas Gainsborough,* London, 1915, p.4.

[22] Anon., 'Mr Gainsborough the Painter,' *Morning Chronicle,* 8 issue 6006, August 1788. The Coyte family referred to is the Rev. William Coyte (1680–1745) who became Rector of Hintlesham in 1709, where he remained until his death. His sons were: William (1708–1775), a physician and botanist; George (1717–1782), a silversmith; Tobias (b.1718); and Beeston (1711–1775), a pastel portrait artist.

Frances Vivares (1709-1780), *Drawing Book of 18 Etchings*, 1739
© Gainsborough's House, Sudbury, Suffolk

been familiar to Gainsborough, particularly if we compare them to his early landscapes. Books such as *A New Book of Landskips, Pleasant and Useful to learn to Draw with out a Master,* drawn by Jean Baptiste Chatelain (1710–58) and published by John Roque (fl.1736–62) in 1737, and a drawing book of 18 etchings by Francis Vivares (1709–80) were recently acquired by Gainsborough's House. Such books of landscapes, which have so much of Gainsborough's early visual vocabulary contained within, were produced in the French-dominated print world of London, which Gainsborough was about to enter. In an etching from such a book depicting a rural landscape with figures, we can see the familiar elements of Dutch-inspired peasant life, with burdock leaves in the foreground, and the crumbling stable and fence, set within very simply ordered pictorial space. It is remarkable when we compare it with Gainsborough's *Wooded Landscape with Old Peasant and Donkeys outside a Barn, Ploughshare and Distant Church* (c.1755–7, recently acquired by Gainsborough's House. The composition and detail of the page from the drawing book is clearly echoed in Gainsborough's

painting, which indicates that from a very early age he was absorbing the pictorial language of landscapes emanating from seventeenth-century Dutch art, which helps to account in part for the sophistication of his paintings so early in his career.

Such sophistication also indicates that the young artist had as good a familiarity with oil paint as he had with drawing. Gainsborough's great supporter Sir Henry Bate Dudley noted the artist had progressed to 'painting several landscapes from the age of ten to twelve,' before 'he quitted Sudbury'.[23]

The Coyte family are also important in Gainsborough's early evolution in being the source of the first account of Tom Peartree. This story, which has been told and retold by many writers, has become one of the fables of Gainsborough's youth, retold in the nineteenth century by Pyne, Cunningham and Fulcher. The settings, always a garden, differ and include the gardens of the Reverend Coyte, Gainsborough's House, and that of Gainsborough's studio in Ipswich. Thomas Peartree is always a thief or

The countryside surrounding Sudbury
© Ron Smith

potential fruit thief, whom Gainsborough depicted. Whether his name relates to his crime or potential crime is difficult to know, but a real Thomas Peartree was buried in All Saints Church in Sudbury in 1740 or 1741 and there were generations of Peartrees in the town. A head of *Tom Peartree* also exists in Christchurch Mansion, Ipswich, dated to the 1750s. The very first account was in an obituary of Gainsborough by an unknown friend, which placed the story in Rev. Coyte's garden though the culprit was not named:

In one of these visits there happened a violent commotion in the family, on account of the Parson's garden having been plundered of a great quantity of wall fruit, and much pains was taken, but without effect, to discover the thief. Young Gainsborough having one summer risen at an early hour, and walked into the garden to make a sketch from an old elm, seated himself in an obscure corner, and had just taken out his chalk to begin, when he observed a fellow's head peeping over the wall of the garden, which was next the road, with

Thomas Gainsborough (1727 - 1788), *Tom Peartree*, c.1750-59, Oil on shaped panel, 38 x 42 cm © Courtesy of Colchester & Ipswich Museums, Ipswich Borough Collection, R.1902-1

Rural Landscape with a man and woman, etching from *A New Book of Landskips, Pleasant and Useful to learn to Draw with out a Master*, drawn by Jean Baptiste Chatelain – and published by John Rocque, 1737, Etching, 110 x 168 mm © The Trustees of the British Museum

Thomas Gainsborough (1727 - 1788), *Wooded Landscape with Old Peasant and Donkeys outside a Barn, Ploughshare and Distant Church*, c.1755, Oil on canvas, 49.5 x 59.7 cm © Gainsborough's House, Sudbury, Suffolk

Thomas Gainsborough
(1727 – 1788), *Cornard Wood, near Sudbury, Suffolk*, 1748, Oil on canvas, 122 x 155 cm
© The National Gallery, London. Bought (Lewis Fund), 1875.

an apparent intention of seeing if the coast was clear. This changed the young Tyro's object, and instead of sketching the elm, he, in a few moments before he was himself observed, made a sketch upon a rough board of the head of the man; and so accurate was the resemblance, that he was instantly known to be a man from the neighbouring village, and upon close enquiry proved to be the fellow who had robbed the garden. This was shewn about the village, and considered as a strong proof of a genius above the common standard.[24]

About a month later Thickenesse recounted the same tale with differences, which he claimed 'Gainsborough related, when I first visited him'.[25] The setting is Gainsborough's garden in Ipswich, which would date the painting to the 1750s, rather than the 1740s in the

first account. The culprit is named as Thomas Peartree and his description matches the painting in Ipswich:

At the bottom of his Ipswich garden, grew a fine bergamot pear tree, and while Mr. Gainsborough his Palate and Brushes in his hand, *Thomas* [Peartree] *was* looking wishfully over the wall, and contemplating how he could come at some of the wind-falls, the sun shone just upon the top of Thomas's nose, and chin, while all the rest of his dejected countenance, appeared in shadow under his broad brimmed hat, which so struck Mr. Gainsborough's fancy (for such are the happy moments for poets and painters) that he snatched up his window shutter, and got *Thomas into his painting room,* before he had even tasted of the forbidden fruit.[26]

Fulcher's account over fifty years later, in the nineteenth century, claimed that the incident took place at Gainsborough's House:

> The house in which Gainsborough was born had a spacious and well-planted orchard annexed to it, and several of the trees are still standing that were there in the Painter's boyhood. Amongst them is the Pear-tree, the robbery of which, as will be hereafter related, furnished his first attempt at portrait painting ... This juvenile effort was preserved for many years, and Gainsborough ultimately made a finished painting of it, under the title of "Tom Peartree's Portrait".

Although we will never be certain of the correct location, almost certainly the story emerges from a real incident, and the identity of Thomas Peartree will undoubtedly remain hazy. In terms of the surviving head in Christchurch Mansion, Ipswich, Thicknesse's account rings true and is the one that, according to Gainsborough's later biographer Whitley, had the most veracity. There is little doubt that whether drawing in his own garden, that of his father or a family friend, it demonstrates both the early ability of Gainsborough and that concentrated drawing time formed an important part of his youth.

As well as drawing, his daily life at this time included his schooling through his maternal uncle the Rev. Humphrey Burrough MA (1689–1757) Master of Sudbury Grammar, which Gainsborough attended from around 1734. Life in Sudbury also meant working within his father's business. The father was for a time a maker of shrouds.

Cornelia Knight (1757–1837) recalled:

> Among the persons of talent I knew, I must not forget Gainsborough. He might be said to be self-taught. I have heard my mother, who knew all about Essex and Suffolk people, say that his father kept a shop, and he was obliged to pink [ornament] shrouds &c. Every spare moment he gave to drawing ... I never saw an artist who had less presumption or vanity.[27]

It is unfortunate that so little appears in Gainsborough's own hand about this period of his early life, apart from a late letter to Henry Bate Dudley prompted by the sale of his *Cornard Wood*, 1748 (National Gallery). 'Mr. Boydell bought the large Landskip [*Cornard Wood*] ...,' Gainsborough wrote, which was 'in some respects a little in the <u>schoolboy</u> stile... this picture was actually painted at Sudbury, in the year 1748: it was begun <u>before I left school;</u> - and was the means of my Father's sending me to London.'[28] Although Gainsborough referred to his great early landscape being painted on his return to his hometown in 1748, he noted how the genesis of the painting, both in his mind and in sketches, had begun in his youth before he left for London.

[23] Bate Dudley, 1788.

[24] Anon., 1788.

[25] Thicknesse, 1788, p.51.

[26] Thicknesse, 1788, p.52.

[27] Cornelia Knight (1757–1837) quoted in Roger Fulford (ed), *The Autobiography of Miss Knight, Lady Companion to Princess Charlotte*, London, 1960, p.31.

[28] Thomas Gainsborough to Henry Bate Dudley 11 March 1788, in John Hayes, *The Letters of Thomas Gainsborough*, London, 2001, no.104.

BECOMING AN ARTIST IN LONDON IN THE 1740s

'... he quitted Sudbury in his thirteenth year, and came to London'

On March 1739 when Gainsborough's paternal uncle Thomas was murdered, he left a will, which concerned much of Gainsborough's close family. Proved on 5 April of the same year it stated that he wanted to continue to help the family: 'I give to Humphrey Gainsborough John Gainsborough Thomas Gainsborough Sarah Gainsborough Susan Gainsborough and Elizabeth Gainsborough six of the children of my brother John Gainsborough Ten Pounds a piece.' This was to be paid to the children at the age of 21, but further to this it made provision for two of the brothers, Gainsborough's elder brother Humphrey whom his uncle had 'some years past taken upon my self the care of ...' and '... who is now in London a pupil at the Academy where Mr Emes is Master in order to be trained up for the Ministry My will is that my executors do pay twenty pounds a year towards defraying the charges that may attend his being trained up as above said for three years from the Date hereof.' For the artist it noted that 'my will is that my executors take care of Thomas Gainsborough another of the sons of my Brother John Gainsborough that he may be brought up to some Light Handy Craft Trade likely to get a comfortable maintenance by and that they do give any sume not exceeding twenty pounds to bind him out to such trade and I leave it to my executors if he shall prove sober and likely to make good use of it to give him ten pounds over and above the ten pounds I have herein given him the better to enable him to set out into the world'.

The will was proved around the time of Gainsborough's twelfth birthday, uncle Thomas's benevolence allowing Gainsborough perhaps to contemplate a brighter future. Although it did not represent hard cash it did mean that he could find 'some Light Handy Craft Trade likely to get a comfortable maintenance by'. The question that followed was where and what. We know from his obituary that 'he quitted Sudbury in his 13th year, and came to London',[29] which presumably means within a year of the will of his uncle and his twelfth birthday, between April 1739 and April 1740. We see that Gainsborough already harboured ambition to become an artist, 'at twelve,' already 'a confirmed painter', and that London was the natural place for him to study.[30] As Thicknesse recalled, ' he went very young to London, where by assistance of his father; the powers of his genius, his modest deportment, and the elegance of his person; he obtained what is called in general, *many friends*'.[31] He was very young, but the family had connections already in London including his brother studying at Moorfields Academy and there were many other connections provided by his father and the Gainsborough family.

He had been encouraged by the Coytes in his drawing and in another account 'an intimate friend of his mothers, being on a visit, was so struck by the merit of several heads he had taken, that he prevailed on his father to allow him to return with him to London, promising that he should remain with him and that he would procure him the best instruction he could obtain.'[32] Gainsborough himself, in a late letter recalled that his early drawings for *Cornard Wood* 'was the means of my Father's sending me to London'.[33]

The consistency in each account is that his talent was recognised early, he was encouraged by his family and family friends and helped by moving to the centre of the art world, London. 'There not being any body in his native country who could properly instruct him in his studies,' an unknown friend recalled 'that he was soon sent to London'.[34]

(Detail of) Anon, An Academy Life Class (possibly St Martin's Lane Academy), c. 1750, sanguine drawing, 478 x 744 mm ©The Trustees of the British Museum

[29] Bate Dudley, 1788.

[30] Cunningham on John Gainsborough (the painter's father). Allan Cunningham, *The Lives of the Most Eminent British Painters*, revised by Mrs. Charles Heaton, London, 1842, vol.1, p.331.

[31] Thicknesse, 1788, pp.7–8.

[32] Sophia Lane, quoted in John Hayes, *The Landscape Paintings of Thomas Gainsborough*, London, 1982, vol.1, p.301.

[33] Thomas Gainsborough to Henry Bate Dudley 11 March 1788, in John Hayes, *The Letters of Thomas Gainsborough*, London, 2001, no.104.

[34] Anon., 1788.

HUBERT GRAVELOT

J. Massard after La Tour, *Portrait of Hubert Gravelot,* 1771, Etching, 180 x 132 mm
© Gainsborough's House, Sudbury, Suffolk

But what did a ' Light Handy Craft Trade,' mean to Gainsborough? The £20 (aside from the further £20) left by his paternal uncle was not a fortune, and the apprenticeships available to him on London were not as wide as one might first imagine. Apprenticeships, normally lasting seven years and begun from around the age of twelve, cost the apprentice a sum of money to embark upon the work and training. To give context to what his inheritance meant it is worth considering two important artists in Gainsborough's life: Francis Hayman (1707/8–1776), who paid £84 for his apprenticeship in 1718 to Robert Browne, history painter; and John Boydell (1720–1804), who paid £50 for his apprenticeship in 1741 to William Henry Toms (c.1700–c.1758), engraver. Being apprentice to a painter was, simply out of the question. On the other hand, most trade apprenticeships at this time cost between £5 and £20, including copperplate engraving and 'Plaister of Paris,' figure makers, but an apprenticeship as a goldsmith and silversmith cost between £20 and £50.[35]

It is recorded by Henry Bate Dudley that when Gainsborough moved to London around 1740 'in his 13th year,' to pursue an artistic career, he first resided with 'a silversmith of some taste', who may also have been a member of the Coyte family.[36] We also know that he was involved with modelling for plaster model shops, but it is uncertain who this was, or whether this was meant to be the start of an apprenticeship. From the evidence we have it does not look like Gainsborough entered upon a formal apprenticeship, or if he did it was short-lived.

Travel to London from Sudbury in mid-eighteenth-century England was not such an onerous

undertaking as one might expect. It formed part of the journey from Ipswich to the capital. In summer coaches went daily [excepting Sunday] and arrived at the Spread Eagle coaching inn on Gracechurch Street, directly next to Leadenhall market. In winter the service was reduced to three days a week (Tuesday, Thursday and Saturday) from the Bull Inn in Bishopsgate, a little further up the street.[37] Given the distance and the stops it might be estimated that the journey would take a long half day or a short full day. It would have been relatively easy for Gainsborough to travel back and forth between London and Sudbury in the 1740s, as writers have long speculated. Arriving at Gracechurch Street in 1740, Gainsborough could easily have been met by his brother who was already established in the City.

His initial residence with 'a silversmith of some taste,' began, possibly in the City. There has been much speculation on the identity of the silversmith, and it is unlikely that we shall ever know it for certain. It may have been a Coyte as Elaine Barr has convincingly speculated.[38] It may have been a Huguenot associate or business, of which we know some were known to the Gainsborough family. What is more certain is that Gainsborough had no intention of becoming a silversmith, even if he had to do some work there initially.

For a young tyro with limited means, the options for developing his natural talent in the London art world included, beyond apprenticeships, work within workshops and businesses, supplemented by training at an academy. Within the London art world in the 1740s, British art was most famously led, as the

[35] Robert Campbell, *The London Tradesman. Being a Compendious View of All the Trades. Professions, Arts, both Liberal and Mechanic, now practised in the Cities of London and Westminster.* London, 1747, pp.334–337.

[36] George Coyte (see previous note) is the silversmith identified as the one Gainsborough stayed with when he first moved to London around 1740 in Elaine Barr, 'Gainsborough and the Silversmith,' *Burlington Magazine*, February 1977, p.113.

[37] *A compleat guide to LONDON, to all persons who have any trade or concern with the city of London and parts adjacent*, Printed for J. Osborn, London, 1740, p.80.

[38] See note 36.

[39] Campbell, 1747, p.113.

[40] George Vertue Notebooks, 1745, in *The Walpole Society*, 1933–34, Vertue III, p.127.

[41] *'The works of the late Edward Dayes: containing An excursion through the principal ... Published 1805 ... Vol 5: Anecdotes of painting in England: with some account of the principal artists, and incidental notes on other arts.'* London, 1805. Edward Dayes (1763–1804), watercolour painter, was born on 6 August 1763 in London. He was apprenticed to the mezzotint engraver and miniaturist William Pether and entered the Royal Academy Schools on 6 October 1780.

[42] Thicknesse, 1788, p.8.

[43] W. Bell Jones (ed.), 'An Autobiography of John Boydell, Engraver', *Flintshire Historical Society Publications*, 1925, vol.11, p.83.

[44] Bate Dudley, 1788.

Anon, An Academy Life Class (possibly St Martin's Lane Academy), c. 1750, sanguine drawing, 478 x 744 mm
©The Trustees of the British Museum

Articles of Apprenticeship of Gainsborough Dupont to Thomas Gainsborough, 12 January 1772
© Gainsborough's House, Sudbury, Suffolk

Tradesman noted by 'the famous Mr. *Hogarth,* whose celebrated Pieces are esteemed all over *Europe'.*[39] It was William Hogarth (1697–1764) who had revived the St Martin's Lane Academy and in 1745 included as teachers 'Mr. Hayman (History Painter &c)' and 'Mr. Gravelot. (designer)',[40] both artists who were directly involved in Gainsborough's training inside and outside the school.

As Edward Dayes stated, it is 'an idle assertion that Gainsborough was self-taught; he studied under Gravelot, with Grignion, and several others, at his house in James Street, Covent Garden, where he had all the means of study that period could afford him.[41] Thicknesse noted that 'by attending a drawing Academy, [Gainsborough] greatly improved his natural talents'.[42] What the Academy offered a student of art was described by Gainsborough's contemporary and colleague, the printmaker John Boydell. He recalled that in this period he 'was advised to draw at the Academy, which would tend more to my improvement than any other method. I went there Five Nights in the Week, the Man sat three nights, a

Women two. The position of the Figures were set by the most noted in the Academy, the Students were admitted at Six o'clock to their places which were all numbered and drawn out of a box, if any vacant places were left the Students might change their situation'.[43]

Boydell then went on to recall that after a drawing session at the Academy he would return home at about 9.30 and then study books on perspective, as this was not taught at the Academy at this point, from which he learned 'the Rules that enabled me to draw Views from Nature'.[44] How Gainsborough learnt perspective is not certain, but is clearly related to his close friendship with the drawing-master Joshua Kirby (1716–1774), which began in the 1740s and included their collaboration on a painting titled *View of St Mary's Church, Hadleigh,* c.1748–50, Hayes 28, private collection which was commissioned by the Reverend Trimmer around 1747. The painting clearly uses the rules of perspective in the depiction of the church and its associated buildings. Kirby gave lectures on perspective at the St. Martin's Lane Academy and published *Dr. Brook Taylor's Method of Perspective Made Easy, both in Theory and Practice* in London in 1754. Proposals for the book had been announced some three years earlier and its bound-in subscription list gives an extraordinary insight into the artistic world that Gainsborough had entered.

According to Bate Dudley: 'Mr. Gravelot, the engraver, was also his patron, and got him introduced at the Old Academy of the Arts, in St. Martin's Lane. He continued to exercise his pencil for some years'.[45] In 1740s London, the production and training in printing, drawing and design was dominated by French artists. The *London Tradesman* of 1747 noted that although 'we have some very good Masters in Design … the best Pieces we have in *England* are executed in *France,* where they excel us much in this Art … I take their Superiority to lie in the Delicacy of the Execution

more than any thing else; and this I attribute to their Workmen being early taught Drawing, which not only helps them in Performance of their Work, but makes them a Judge of what they are about'.[46] The French influence led many burgeoning artists to take time to learn French to advance their studies including Gainsborough's colleague Boydell:

In order to have some knowledge of French, I began with Telemachus in French I did not then understand on word; by learning some phrases in the Grammar and by the help of the Dictionary. Before I got to the end, I understood a great deal; but I found myself at a great loss in regard to the pronunciation and understanding any discourse I heard; happening to go by a Foreign Chapel at St. James's on a Sunday I found a service according to the liturgy of the Church of England and a

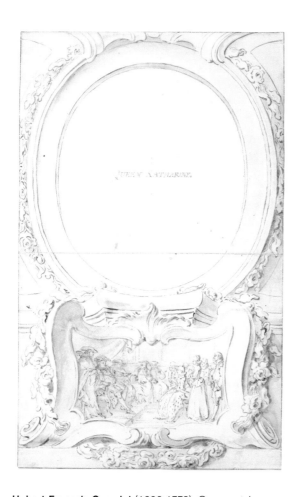

Hubert-Francois Gravelot (1699-1773), *Ornamental Surround for a Portrait of Katherine of Aragon,* c.1743, Pen and black ink with sepia wash and touches of red chalk on paper © Gainsborough's House, Sudbury, Suffolk

Houbraken (1698-1780), Jacobus after Arthur Pond (1701-1758) and Hubert Francois Gravelot (1699-1773), *Katherine of Aragon, Queen of K. Henry VIII.* (From The Heads of Illustrious Persons in Great Britain', 1743), 1743, Engraving © Gainsborough's House, Sudbury, Suffolk

Sermon Preached every Sunday in French. I got a Prayer Book - and heard the Clergyman pronounce every word distinctly, by accustoming myself to follow him mot a mot I learnt more than I could in any other manner, I always attended for a length of time and by degrees accustomed myself to speak and writ the Language which enabled me to Correspond with Foreigners- which was of great service to me.[47]

Most prominent amongst his mentors and the influences that Gainsborough experienced after his arrival in London was Hubert-François Gravelot (formerly Bourguignon, 1699–1773), better known simply as Gravelot. The French artist had moved to London around 1732, where he remained until 1745, with three separate studio addresses in Covent Garden.[48] When Gainsborough joined his studio in the early 1740s, Gravelot was operating at the sign of the Mortar and Pestle. There appeared to be no formal apprenticeship as such and Gainsborough's role appears to have been a paid one, working alongside the printmakers, Charles Grignion (bap.1721, d.1810) and Thomas Major (1720–1799). Major and more particularly Grignion engraved many of Gravelot's drawings. Grignion later observed that Gravelot was essentially a draughtsman: 'Gravelot was a designer, but could not engrave. He etched a great deal in what is called the manner of Painters etchings, but did not know the graver'.[49] Gravelot was the 'ingenious draughtsman', who taught design at the St Martin's Lane Academy, designing book illustrations as well as metalwork and ceramics. The position for Gainsborough was different from his colleagues in the studio, for like Gravelot his ability lay in draughtsmanship not etching and Gainsborough's first recorded print is not until around 1754, for Kirby's

book on perspective: he appears not to have been employed as an engraver, but as a draughtsman. *The Morning Chronicle* later recorded concerning Gravelot: 'under whose instructions he drew most of the ornaments which decorate the illustrious heads so admirably engraved by Houbraken.'[50] Much of Gainsborough's own collection of paintings, drawings, prints and books were sold after either his or his wife's death (in 1799). These included volumes that were very important to his early life and career including *Birch's Lives of Illustrious Persons, with the heads of Houbraken*, and Kirby on perspective.[51]

Gainsborough must have acquired a lot of new skills through Gravelot. Most important was his development as a draughtsman, and acquiring the ability to produce drawings that were to be made into prints. Certainly, given his financial circumstances, drawing would have been an important source of income to the young artist. There is a later account of his early sale of drawings by the Huguenot Panton Betew (1722–1799, a corruption of his baptismal name, Pantin Buteux), who came from a well-known family of silversmiths and was known to sell early drawings: 'I have had many and many a drawing of his [Gainsborough] in my shop-window before he went to Bath. Ay, and he has often been glad to receive seven or eight shillings from me for what I have sold: Paul Sandby knows it well'.[52]

We know Gainsborough created drawings for Gravelot, but he also did so for the printmakers of his own generation. Boydell bought four drawings from Gainsborough in 1747, with the intention 'to stay in the Country the Summer following,' his marriage on 1 January 1748, 'that I might not lose any time I brought four Copper Plates with me, and four neat

[45] Bate Dudley, 1788.

[46] Campbell, 1747, p.113.

[47] Bell Jones, 1925, vol.11, p.84.

[48] The sign of the Mortar and Pestle, the Golden Cup in King Street and later James Street.

[49] *The Farington Diary*, 1 July 1806. From a typescript in the British Museum, quoted in John Hayes, *Gainsborough as Printmaker*, London, 1972, p.2. The diary is published in full as Kenneth Garlick and Alexander MacIntyre (eds), *The Diary of Joseph Farington*, 16 vols., New Haven and London, 1978.

[50] Anon., 1788.

[51] Sale of 11 May 1799 at Christie's from Gainsborough's collection: '105 Kirby's perspective…102 Birch's Lives of Illustrious Persons, with the heads of Houbraken…'

[52] Betew quoted in John Thomas Smith, *Nollekens and his Times*, London, 1828, p.175.

[53] Bell Jones,1925, vol. 11. p.86.

[54] *General Advertiser*, 24 December 1748. I am grateful to Mark Hallett and Peter Moore for this advertisement.

John Boydell (1720-1804), after Thomas Gainsborough (1727-1788), *A View near to Ipswich in Suffolk*, 1748, Etching and engraving, 24.9x34.2 cm © Gainsborough's House, Sudbury, Suffolk

John Boydell (1720-1804), after Thomas Gainsborough (1727-1788), *Drawn after Nature*, after 1751, Etching and engraving © Gainsborough's House, Sudbury, Suffolk

Drawings by Gainsborough which I engraved before the Summer began after which I took several Views … I likewise made Drawings …'.[53]

Boydell was anxious to develop his print business, which at this time focused upon topographical series. He returned to London in the autumn of 1748 and published the prints he had been working on, including the plates from the Gainsborough drawings. Published in late 1748, they were advertised in the newspaper as 'Four views after Nature; being Prospects near Ipswich in Suffolk; curiously engraved… Price 2s the Set'.[54] The first editions of these prints are rare, and have very different lettering from the later editions. They are interesting because they were primarily being sold as topographical views, but although they bear some relationship to the landscape surrounding Ipswich, they are essentially fashionable depictions owing far more to models of existing pictures than fidelity to viewpoints. Stylistically, they bear a resemblance to

both Gainsborough and Boydell. Boydell knew that topography was saleable and they, as the advert indicates, bear the title, *A View near to Ipswich in Suffolk*. Interesting too is the fact that the prints acknowledge Boydell twice, as publisher and engraver, but no mention of Gainsborough appears on the print. In 1751, Boydell moved to larger premises with a shop with the sign of a Unicorn at the corner of Queen Street in Cheapside. Here the prints were re-issued on more than one occasion with the Cheapside address and the name of Gainsborough appeared on them, as the name of Gainsborough meant more to his market than the topography around Ipswich. They were also newly titled as *Drawn After Nature,* with the topographical title removed.

When Gainsborough had first arrived in London 'he had not formed any high Ideas of his own powers, but rather considered himself as one, among a crowd of young Artists, who might be able in a country town

The Old Horse, plaster model of a horse, c.1740
© Private collection on loan to Gainsborough's House, Suffolk
Once owned by the artist John Constable (1776-1837)

Thomas Gainsborough
(1727-1788), Figure
modelled by Gainsborough
for his picture *The
Woodman*, reproduced in
William T Whitley, Art Notes,
The Collector Magazine IX
no. 34, March 1930
© Gainsborough's House,
Sudbury, Suffolk

(by turning his hand to every kind of painting) pick up a decent livelihood'.[55] As a result another aspect of Gainsborough's training, no doubt linked to his need to earn his living, was model making, employed in 'plaister' shops that created models for ornamenting and decorating interiors, which were a growing business in London and reached their zenith between 1760 and 1825.[56] His friend recalled that just after he was 'sent to London…' he 'made his first essays in art, by modelling figures of cows, horses, and dogs, in which he attained very great excellence: there is a call in the plaister shops from an old horse that he modelled, which has peculiar merit'.[57]

Gainsborough famously used models in creating his paintings and this early experience helped him to develop quite a facility for this, which is confirmed by Smith who recalled Nollekens instructing Gainsborough on modelling a Pomeranian dog from terracotta, which he gave to him as a gift:

> … 'your thumbs ; thumb it about till you get it into shape.' ' What,' said Gainsborough, 'in this manner ?' having taken up a bit of clay, and looking at a picture of Abel's Pomeranian Dog which hung over the chimney-piece this way ?' Yes,' said Nollekens; ' you'll do a great deal more with your thumbs.'

---

[55] Thicknesse, 1788, p.8.

[56] Timothy Clifford, 'The plaster shops of the rococo and neo-classical era in Britain, in *Journal of the History of Collections*, 1992, vol. 4, issue 1, pp.39–65.

[57] Anon., 1788. A plaster model of an old horse once owned by John Constable is on permanent display at Gainsborough's House, Sudbury.

[58] Smith, 1828, p.173.

[59] The catalogue includes the following lots: '11. Three mannequins with all their movements in copper and made in England two feet high for draping and for drawing strong figures.

12. Various garments of different fabrics serving the said mannequins.'

[60] See William T. Whitley, Art Notes, *The Collector*, March 1930, vol. IX, no.34, p.148.

[61] Burnet, 1842, p.244.

Thomas Gainsborough RA (1727 - 1788), *View of St Mary's Church, Hadleigh*, c. 1748, Oil on canvas, 190.5 x 91.4 cm
©Philip Mould Ltd

Mr. Gainsborough, by whom I was standing, observed to me : ' You enjoyed the music, my little fellow, and I am sure you long for this model ; there, I will give it to you ' and I am delighted with it still. I have never had it baked, fearing it might fly in the kiln, as the artist had not kneaded the clay well before he commenced working it, and I conclude that the model must still contain a quantity of fixed air.[58]

In his portrait paintings, Gainsborough very clearly used lay figures, a practice he was exposed to within Gravelot's studio, and a fact recorded in his letters and evident particularly in his early work. After the designer's death, his Paris studio sale of 19 May 1773 included lots 11 and 12, which describe three English mannequins, jointed in copper with various costumes.[59]

Further accounts of his making and using figures of a lady and even a woodman are recorded.[60] The ease with which he had learnt to make figures

undoubtedly aided this method, something he took further in creating landscapes in three dimensions. Reynolds recalled of Gainsborough, 'He even framed a kind of model of landscapes on his table; composed of broken stones, dried herbs, and pieces of looking-glass, which he magnified and improved into rocks, trees, and water'.[61]

How Gainsborough developed as a painter owed less to the French influence in this period than it did to the Dutch Old Masters and the burgeoning British School of painting in London in 1740s. There is also the question of approaches to landscape and portrait painting, which are very different disciplines and developed at different paces within Gainsborough's work. In landscape painting, Gainsborough initially looked to seventeenth-century Dutch painters, most notably Jan Wijnants (active 1643; d.1684) and Jacob van Ruisdael (1628/9?–1682), and within portraiture he looked to the British School, most notably Francis Hayman and William Hogarth.

J Osborn, *A Compleat Guide to London*, 1740
© Gainsborough's House, Sudbury, Suffolk
Showing how relatively easy it was to travel
between Sudbury and London

Stockton car. Bear, Bafinghall ftr.
M.

Stone car. Axe, Aldermanbury, T;
Caftle, Wood ftr. M; Bloffom's
Inn, Lawrence lane, M.W;
Caftle and Falcon, Alderfgate,
M.T.

Stone-houfe car. King's Head, Old
Change, W.F.

Stonington car. Queen's Head,
Southwark, F.

Stony-ftratford car. Rofe and Crown,
St. John's ftr. F; George, Alderfgate ftr. T.F.

Stourbridge car. Saracen's Head,
Snow-hill, M.S; Caftle and Fal-
con, Alderfgate ftr. M. Th;
George, Snow-hill, T; White
Horfe, Friday ftr. M.W.F.

Stourton [Great] car. Swan with
Two Necks, St. John's ftr. W.

Stowe in-the-world car. Bear and
Ragged Staff, Smithfield, Th.

Stowe car. Saracen's Head, Snow-
hill, Th.

Stowe-market car. Spread Eagle,
Graffchurch ftr. Th.

Stratford [Effex] car. Saracen's
Head and Bell, within Aldgate,
M.

Stratford and Bow co. Whitechapel
Bars, every Day often.

Stratford-on-avon car. Ram, Smithfield, Th; Pack-horfes there,
Th; Saracen's Head, Snow-
hill, F.

Stratford [Stony] car. Rofe and
Crown, St. John's, ftreet, F;
George, Alderfgate ftr. T.F.

Stretham car. Four Swans, Bifhop-
gate ftr. W.Th.F.

Stretham [Surrey] car. Horfefhoe,
Blackman ftr. Southwark, where
Teams and Coaches call every
Day.

Stroud [Kent] co. Spread Eagle,
Graffchuch ftr. T.Th.S. Summer, M.W.F. Winter.

Stroud-water, and Places adjacent,
car. George, Snow-hill, F;
King's Head, Old Change, W.
F.

Stuckley car. Bear and Ragged
Staff, Smithfield, M.

Sudbury car. Spread Eagle, Graffchurch ftr. Th.
——co. Spread Eagle there, T.Th.
S; Bull, within Bifhopfgate, T.
Th.S.

Sunderidge car. Talbot, Southwark,
T.F.

Sunderland car. Bear, Bafinghall
ftr.; White Horfe, Cripplegate,
M.

Suttle car. Caftle, Wood ftr. F.

Sutton car. Horfefhoe, Blackman
ftr.; Teams and Coaches every
Day.

Swaffham car. Vine, Bifhopfgate,
T; Green Dragon there, W.
Th.F.

Swallowfield car. Bull, Holbourn,
M. once a Fortnight; King's
Arms, Holbourn Bridge, F.

Swamborough car. Bell, Warwick
lane, W.

Swanfey car. George, Snow-hill, S.

Swindon [Wilts] car. Saracen's
Head, Snow-hill, F; King's
Arms, Holbourn Bridge, S;
calls at the White Horfe Cellar
and White Bear, Piccadilly.

Sydenham co. Old Catharine Wheel,
Bifhopfgate ftr. every Day in
Summer.

T.

Tadcafter car. Red Lion, Alderfgate ftr. M; Bear, Bafinghall
ftr. F; White Horfe, Cripplegate, M.

Tamworth car. Caftle and Falcon,
Alderfgate ftr. M.T; George
there, M.

Tamworth co. Saracen's Head,
Snow-hill, F.

Taunton car. Bell, Wood ftr. S.
——co. Saracen's Head, Friday ftr.
T.

Tedbury car. Bell, Friday ftr. T.
W.F; King's Arms, Holbourn
Bridge, S; Rofe there, W;
George, Snow-hill, Th. S;
King's Head, Old Change, F.

Tedington car. Windmill, St. John's
ftr. S.

Tedwell car. Bloffom's Inn, Lawrence lane, Th.

L 2   Teefon

(Detail of)
Thomas Gainsborough
(1727-1788), *Wooded
Landscape with
Herdsman Seated*, 1746
– 1747, Oil on canvas,
49x65.5 cm
© Gainsborough's
House, Sudbury, Suffolk

'... MY FIRST IMITATIONS OF LITTLE DUTCH LANDSKIPS'

In 1772, on the eve of his permanent move to London, Thomas Gainsborough had established himself as one of the greatest portrait painters of his age. In the same year, the gossipy *Town and Country* magazine pointed out that it had not always been the case, stating of the great artist's early life: "I remember him some years ago … when he was only a landscape painter, and merely as such must have starved – he did not sell six pictures a year'.[62] As one of the very few contemporary insights into his early practice, it is an interesting account recalling that Gainsborough's earliest paintings and drawings were of landscapes, an art form through which he developed before he established himself as a portrait painter. An obituary of the artist recalled that his 'first efforts were small landscapes, which he frequently sold to dealers at trifling prices'.[63]

According to Bate Dudley, Gainsborough had begun painting in Sudbury before he moved to London: 'From delineation he got to colouring; and after painting several landscapes from the age of ten to twelve, he quitted Sudbury'.[64] This is consistent with the Reverend Kirby Trimmer's recollections of his earliest paintings having had a Dutch influence:

> As is well known, Gainsborough was liberal in giving away his productions, and Joshua Kirby came in for the lion's share … his first sketch in oils, sold at my father's sale, after the manner of Waterloo, whom in his early days he much studied; and I have now Waterloo's etching, given by Gainsborough to Kirby. He also gave him above a hundred drawings in pencil and chalk, most of which I still have; six or seven small landscapes in oil … so that my family possessed the best collection of his early or Suffolk productions I have seen.[65]

Gainsborough's debt to Dutch painting has long been acknowledged, by the artist himself, and by his contemporaries and later writers on the artist. 'I feel such a fondness for my first imitations of little Dutch

Thomas Gainsborough RA
(1727-1788), Holywells Park, Ipswich, 1748–1750, Oil on canvas, 48.5 x 65 cm
© Courtesy of Colchester & Ipswich Museums, Ipswich Borough Collection, R.1992-5

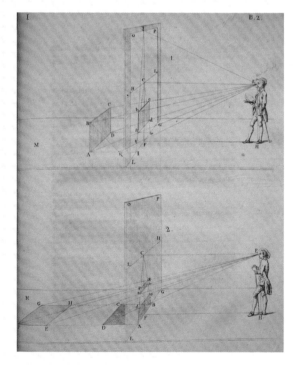

Joshua Kirby (1716 – 1774), Illustration of figure thought to be Gainsborough, *Dr. Brook Taylor`s Method of Perspective made easy; Both in Theory and Practice:...*, Published London, 1768
© Gainsborough's House, Sudbury, Suffolk

Jacob Isaackszoon van Ruisdael (1628-82), *Foret*, 17th Century, Oil on canvas, 171 x 194cm
©Douai (France), Musee de la Chartreuse Photographe : Hugo Martens

landskips,' he wrote.[66] The debt is beyond question, but it has to be asked how Gainsborough learnt the method so well, how he was exposed to Dutch art, and how he absorbed it so completely.[67] 'The first master he studied was Wynants,' wrote a friend in the *Morning Chronicle* of 1788, 'whose thistles and dock-leaves he has frequently introduced into his early pictures. The next was Ruysdael; but his colouring is less sombre ... He has sometimes very happily seized upon the best manner of Teniers ... Of the animals of Snyders he thought with admiration, and seems to have made that master his model'.[68] There was a great taste and interest for seventeenth-century Dutch painting in London in the middle of the eighteenth century, and many paintings, copies and prints were available through the growing art market. Gainsborough's exposure to painting in the 1740s and those by Wijnants and Ruisdael came through both direct and indirect contact.

The early drawing books he saw in the 1730s contained the vocabulary of Dutch painting. Chatelain's etching from *A New Book of Landskips* shows the characteristic dock and burdock leaves that became *motifs* in Gainsborough's early landscape paintings. At this time too, many of Gainsborough's printmaking colleagues were making etchings from Dutch paintings and drawings, such as *A Set of Sheep after Berghem*, etched by Boydell in 1746, one of his earliest productions when he set up his business on the Strand. When Christie's sold off much of Gainsborough's collection in 1799 it contained prints and drawings by his beloved Dutch masters.[69]

Gainsborough undoubtedly learnt through copying examples of Dutch painting, in print, through copies and through the original. His black and white chalk drawing of a Ruisdael painting, *La Forêt,* now in the Whitworth Gallery in Manchester, shows that he did

Thomas Gainsborough RA
(1727-1788), *A Wooded
Landscape with a River,
Cattle and Figures*, after
Jacob van Ruisdael, 1746-
1747, Paper (Buff)
Chalk (Black); Chalk (White),
409 x 423 mm
© Courtesy of the
Whitworth, The University of
Manchester

copy in detail and that at the very least was exposed to a very fine copy, if not to the original itself.[70]

The most intriguing reference to Gainsborough's direct contact with Dutch painting is contained in Ellis Waterhouse's book of 1958 on the artist, in which he noted that he 'kept up this self-taught method of study during his early years in London by repairing pictures for the art trade, for an unusually candid sale catalogue of 1762 (of Mr Oldfield's pictures) has the entries: 17. *A Dutch landscape, repaired by Mr*

---

[62] Anon., *The Town and Country Magazine or Universal Repository of Knowledge, Instruction, and Entertainment*, 1772, vol. IV, p.486.

[63] Anon., 1788.

[64] Bate Dudley, 1788.

[65] Rev. Kirby Trimmer quoted in Walter Thornbury, *The Life of J M W Turner, R.A.*, London 1862, vol.2, p.58.

[66] Thomas Gainsborough to Thomas Harvey 22 May 1788, in Hayes, 2001, no.108, p.174.

[67] See Susan Foister, 'Young Gainsborough and the English taste for Dutch landscape', and Rica Jones, 'Gainsborough's materials and methods', both in Susan Foister, Rica Jones and Olivier Mesley, exhibition catalogue, *Young Gainsborough*, London, National Gallery in association with *Apollo*, 1997.

[68] Anon., 1788.

[69] Sale of 11 May 1799, Christie's from Gainsborough's collection: '100…. Ditto of animals by Ridinger… (sold for £2); 98 A book containing a quantity of fine etching, by C. du Jardin, Waterloo, Bergham, &c… (sold for 9 guineas); 93 A book of fifty-four drawings of shipping, in Indian ink, by V. de Velde, exceedingly fine…'' (sold for 3 guineas); 99 A book of 18 fine prints, from Wouvermans (sold for £2).'

[70] *Landscape after Ruisdael's 'La Forêt'*. Black and white chalks on paper, 408 x 424 mm, Whitworth Art Gallery, University of Manchester.

Thomas Gainsborough (1727-1788), *Wooded Landscape with Herdsman Seated*, 1746 – 1747, Oil on canvas, 49x65.5 cm
© Gainsborough's House, Sudbury, Suffolk

Gainsborough. 56. Wynants, a landscape, the figures by Mr Gainsborough. But this is the only aspect of his art which he taught himself.'[71] Until now there was uncertainty about this reference and identity of Mr Oldfield, as the catalogue that Waterhouse saw has not been found. Mr John Oldfield (d.1768), it is now clear, was a writing master resident at Tufton Street, Westminster, known as a collector and connoisseur of paintings. 'He is not only a good judge of *writing*, but also a connoisseur in *painting*,' wrote W. Massey in 1763 and he is listed as buying work at the sale of Mr John van Spangen after his death in 1748.[72] Gainsborough's connection with Oldfield may have been through him being a writing master, a provider of training that was part of an artist's and draughtsman's education. We know that he was a subscriber to Kirby's perspective, and that Gainsborough had a very fine copperplate hand. In his early years, Gainsborough turned his artistic abilities to many branches, which is not surprising given his growing reputation as a landscape painter. Such direct involvement with Dutch painting must have aided his understanding of painting as well as his ability to add convincing figures within paintings of this period.

His debt to Dutch painting is clearly apparent, even in scenes very clearly evocative of his native Suffolk. Using the vocabulary of Dutch painting and the works inspired by that taste in the period, Gainsborough was beginning to develop his own voice. At times Gainsborough was necessarily topographical if he was involved in a commission, like Hadleigh Church, the pools at Holywell and the land in *Mr and Mrs Andrews.*

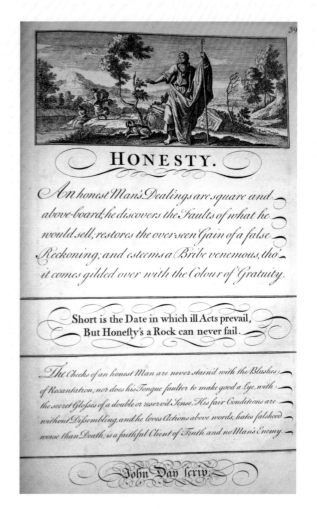

Mr John Oldfield in George Bickham's (died 1749),
The Universal Penman, or the Art of Writing made useful …,
London, H. Overton, 1743
© Gainsborough's House, Sudbury, Suffolk

---

[71] Thomas Ellis Waterhouse, *Gainsborough*, London, 1913, p.13.
[72] W. Massey, *The Origin and Progress of Letters*, London, 1763, p.113.

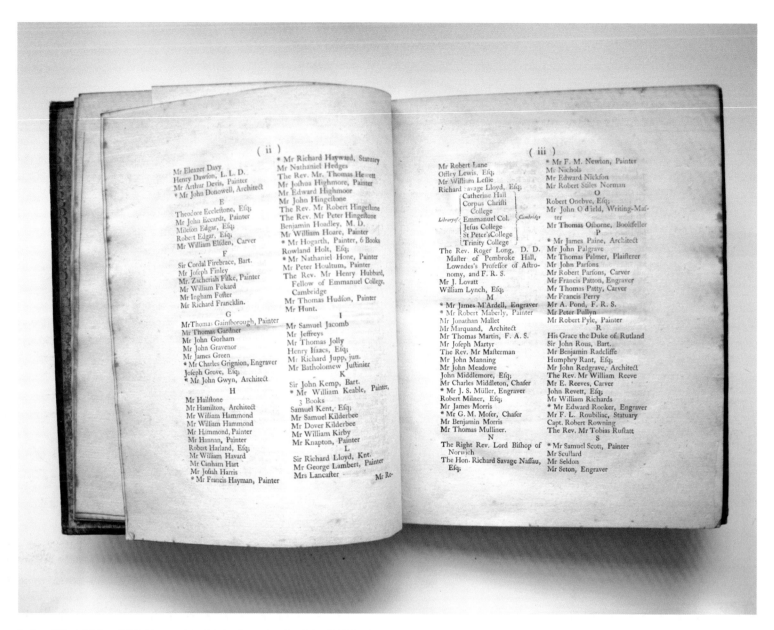

Joshua Kirby (1716 – 1774), Perspective of Subcribers showing John Oldfield, drawing master from *Dr. Brook Taylor`s Method of Perspective made easy; Both in Theory and Practice:...*, Published London, 1768

Mr Oldfield, Drawing Master, was a collector of Dutch paintings and employed Gainsborough to work on them.

(Detail of)
Thomas Gainsborough
(1727-1788),
*A Gentleman with a
Dog in a Wood*, 1746,
Oil on canvas,
66.6x50.1 cm
© Private collection on
loan to Gainsborough's
House, Suffolk

'... - A PORTRAIT PAINTER - WHICH HE IS IN THE TRUEST SENSE OF THE WORD...'

When Gainsborough first moved to London his experience was in landscape painting, and then his drawing was developed through Gravelot and the St Martin's Lane Academy. A friend of Gainsborough recalled that he, 'afterwards engaged in portraits, his price was from three to five guineas: but, as he expanded his fame, he advanced his prices ...' Rather dismissively his friend concluded that 'his early portraits have very little to recommend them'.[73] Whether we agree or not, there is little doubt that his sophistication as a landscape painter preceded his sophistication as a portrait painter. We know that he was employed, for example, repairing Dutch landscapes for the art trade and the landscape backgrounds to portraits by other artists.

The move to portraiture was a natural and necessary development. We are told that he had a natural talent for portraiture that was discovered by others, and that an 'intimate friend of his mothers ... [was] so struck by the merit of several heads he had taken,'.[74] The *Town*

and Country magazine pointed out 'by a way of amusement, he painted the heads of a few of his acquaintances: the likeness was too perfect not to strike every one.'[75] To be a rounded painter and to forge a living, it was essential to paint at least adequate portraits. If his first efforts, 'had little to recommend them,' it demonstrates both that Gainsborough had to learn this art and that the British School of portraiture was still in its infancy.

Gainsborough's training at the St Martin's Lane Academy was focused upon the figure, as Boydell recounted. The Academy did not focus exclusively on drawing, however, but also taught painting, as we know from the list of Masters provided by George Vertue in 1745: 'For the study of Drawing this winter at the Academy of Painting & Sculpture kept in St. Martins Lane – Charing X. an advertisement that on Saturday even. 7.28 will meet at the half moon Tavern in the Strand – to take Subscriptions for the following winter Mr. Hayman (History Painter &c) Mr. Gravelot.

Anonymous, *A Perspective View of the Grand Walk in Vauxhall Gardens, and the Orchestra*, 1765, Etching © Gainsborough's House, Sudbury, Suffolk Hayman and Gravelot were both involved in the decorative schemes of Vauxhall Gardens, which also included contributions from Gainsborough.

A Perspective View of the Grand Walk in Vauxhall Gardens and the Orchestra.

Francis Hayman (1708–1776), *Francis Hayman; Grosvenor Bedford*, c. 1748-1750, Oil on canvas, 71.8 x 91.4 cm
© National Portrait Gallery, London

(designer) Mr. Moser (chaser) Mr. Rubilliac (Statuary.) Mr. Yeo. (Seal Graver) Mr…. (Landskip painter) Mr. Wills (portrait painter Treasurer)'.[76]

Gainsborough also learnt the elegant Rococo line from Gravelot. For mentoring in painting, he had Gravelot's great friend and drinking companion Francis Hayman as one of his early painting mentors. The painter Edward Edwards (1738–1806) wrote in his memoirs of artists that, 'at a proper age he [Gainsborough] was sent to London, and placed under the tuition of Mr. Hayman, with whom he, however, staid but a short time'. He added a note to this on the advice of Grignion 'who was intimately acquainted with the painter in his youth,' noting that 'Mr. Gainsborough received his first instructions in the rudiments of art from Mr. Gravelot'.[77] Gravelot and Hayman were not only friends, but close artistic associates working together on a number of illustrations and even on designs for Vauxhall Gardens supper boxes, a project that Gainsborough was almost certainly involved in.[78]

How the mentoring worked with Hayman is difficult to know, but there is clear evidence that Gainsborough carried out work for Hayman under his direction, leading us to assume that it was a similar relationship to that with Gravelot. Gainsborough's obvious ability was used to assist way beyond the purely mechanical: in this case it involved painting landscape backgrounds for his 'pictures in little,' or conversation pieces are they are now more familiarly known.[79] In a letter to his patron Grosvenor Bedford (1708–1771), concerning his portrait of Bedford's children,

[73] Anon, 1772, vol. IV, p.486.
[74] Sophia Lane, quoted in Hayes, 1982, vol.1, p.301.
[75] Anon., 1772, vol, IV, p.486.
[76] Vertue Notebooks, 1933–34, Vertue III, 1745 p.127.
[77] Edward Edwards, *Anecdotes of Painters who have resided or Been born in England*, London, 1808, p.130.
[78] See Lawrence Gowing, 'Hogarth, Hayman and the Vauxhall Decorations', *Burlington Magazine*, January 1953, vol.XCV, pp.4–19, where it is suggested that Gainsborough might have helped with the decorations. The attribution of prints after the decorations illustrates clearly the working relationship of Hayman and Gravelot
[79] See Brian Allen, *Francis Hayman*, London, 1987, pp.39–40, and Susan Foister, Rica Jones and Olivier Mesley (eds), *Young Gainsborough*, exh. cat., London, National Gallery, 1997.
[80] Quoted in Allen, 1987, p.92.

Thomas Gainsborough (1727-1788), *A Gentleman with a Dog in a Wood*, 1746, Oil on canvas, 66.6x50.1 cm
© Private collection on loan to Gainsborough's House, Suffolk

Francis Hayman (1708–1776), *Portrait of Elizabeth and Charles Bedford*, (1746-7), Oil on canvas, 76.2 x 63.5 cm © Private collection Gainsborough was employed by Hayman to paint the landscape in this portrait.

Hayman wrote: 'I have an opportunity of getting the landscape done by Gainsborough whilst he is in Town.'[80] The painting *Portrait of Elizabeth and Charles Bedford,* (1746–7, private collection) contains a landscape typical of Gainsborough.

These domestic scale portraits set within a landscape provided a lucrative opportunity for Gainsborough to exercise his already manifest ability as a landscape painter. As his friend noted,'his first efforts were small landscapes, which he frequently sold to the dealers at trifling prices,' before developing as a portrait artist.[81] Within his own early portrait practice, the influence of Hayman is extremely apparent. Take, for example, the figure in the portrait supposedly of *Philip Thicknesse* of early 1750s (Saint Louis Museum of Art, Missouri,

USA) and many others which adopt the stance with a raised leg. This characteristic pose was used by Gainsborough in his portrait of John Plampin, c.1752 (National Gallery, London) and as a figure in the foreground of *Languard Fort*.[82] Gainsborough learnt from Hayman the practicalities of painting figures and drapery.[83] The fact that Hayman employed Gainsborough to paint the backgrounds in some of his paintings indicates his competence in painting landscapes. This raises the question as to their working relationship, with one an established master, the other a developing but independent artist. According to a reviewer in the mid nineteenth century the master-pupil relationship was limited and short-lived: 'He also became a pupil of Hayman, but after a short and unprofitable residence with him he hired a room with a Mr. Jorden.'[84] This was for Gainsborough to set up his own practice as both landscape and portrait painter.

Francis Hayman
(1708–1776), *Portrait of a Gentleman*, c.1750, Oil on canvas, 63.5 x 76.5 cm © Saint Louis Art Museum, Museum Purchase 73:1945

[81] Anon., 1788.

[82] This lost work is known through a print in the collection of Gainsborough House.

[83] See Brian Allen, 'Francis Hayman at *Gainsborough's House,' Gainsborough's House Society Annual report 1989/90*, pp.27–34.

[84] J. M. [probably John Mitford, d.1859] editor of the *Gentleman's Magazine*, 1856, review of Fulcher, p.199.

Thomas Gainsborough
(1727-1788), *John Plampin*,
About 1752, Oil on canvas,
50.2 x 60.3 cm
© The National Gallery,
London. Bequeathed by
Percy Moore Turner, 1951.

Thomas Major (1720-1799), after Thomas
Gainsborough (1727-1788), *(Detail of)
Land-Guard Fort in Suffolk*, 1754, Etching
and engraving, 39.4 x 59.4
© Gainsborough's House, Sudbury, Suffolk

PERSONAL LIFE: SUCCESS AND TRAGEDY

Gainsborough's move to London came through the support of his close family and the patronage of his uncle. It is clear why Gainsborough's older brother Humphrey had found favour from an uncle who was an ardent dissenter with strong religious conviction. Such conviction is illustrated in his funding of the dissenting chapel in Sudbury and reflected in his funding of Humphrey's training to be a minister in London at the Moorfields Academy 'where Mr Eames is Master.' In Gainsborough's case his uncle's patronage is not as clear, although by all accounts a bright, talented and pleasant boy might easily have found favour with his uncle. One thing does seem certain is that if Gainsborough had shown no religious inclination, nor followed the dissenting worship of his uncle, he was unlikely to have found such favour.

Initially it is likely that Gainsborough worshiped in a dissenting chapel in London and lived in the City as opposed to Westminster. This is where the majority of his family and associates lived, and where he ended up living after his marriage in 1746. It is also where the majority of silversmiths set up at this time. Bate Dudley recalled that 'The person at whose house he principally resided was a silversmith of some taste; and from him he was ever ready to confess he derived great assistance'.[85] If he had an apprenticeship, it would have included accommodation, although it seems that Gainsborough did not enter upon any such formal agreement or if he did it was very short-lived, as the usual term would have been seven years.

There is no evidence that he stayed in the City of London, as his early training and his development as an artist almost exclusively took place in Westminster, and any connections that he made through worship were through Anglican churches rather than the dissenting meeting houses which proved the most helpful to him in his future career. His wife-to-be Margaret Burr (1727–1798) was, according to their marriage records, part of the congregation of St George's, Hanover Square. This was famously the church of George Frederic Handel (1685–1759) and its Rector was Andrew Trebeck (1681–1759), who had been instrumental in excommunicating Alexander Keith, in whose nearby chapel the Gainsboroughs were later to be married.[86]

Thicknesse wrote about Gainsborough's wife and marriage with an accuracy that was only proved to be correct relatively recently.[87] He recalled that when Gainsborough 'obtained his nineteenth year, he met with a very pretty Scots girl, of low birth who by the luck of the day* had an annuity settled upon her for life of two hundred pounds a year, to this girl he offered his hand and heart, which perhaps no other woman of any fortune would at that time have refused ...
*No reflection is meant here on Mrs. Gainsborough's virtue.'[88]

In the churchyard at Kew, Thomas Gainsborough is buried next to his wife Margaret. The inscription indicates that she died exactly ten years after her husband at the age of 71, being born in the same year as he. The records of St James, Piccadilly, Westminster, indicate that she was born on 7 October 1727 and baptised Margaret Burr there just over a week later on 15 October.[89] Her parents were recorded as William and Margaret Burr, although as Thicknesse knew, 'she had an annuity settled upon her for life,' due to her being the illegitimate daughter of Henry Somerset, 3rd Duke of Beaufort (1707–1745). Documents at the Beaufort estate at Badminton state that 'from and after the decease of the said Duke for and during the natural Life of her the said Margaret Burr Paiable and to be paid in and upon the Twenty fifth day of December and Twenty fifth day of June yearly ...'.[90] The Duke's

(Detail of)
Thomas Gainsborough
(1727-1788),
The Charterhouse,
1748, Oil on canvas,
55.8 x 55.8 cm
© Coram in the care of
the Foundling Museum

[85] Bate Dudley, 1788.
[86] Andrew Trebeck DD (1681–1759) was Rector of St George's from 1727 to 1759. He was educated at Charterhouse and Christ Church, Oxford.
[87] Susan Sloman, 'Margaret Gainsborough, 'A Prince's Daughter',' *Gainsborough's House Review*, 1995/6, pp.47–55, and David Tyler, 'Searching for Mrs Gainsborough,' Ye *Gainsborough News*, 1997, vol.10, pp.100–105.
[88] Thicknesse, 1788, pp.8–9.
[89] FHL Film Number: 1042308, Reference ID: 2:2RLD2CR
[90] Quoted in Sloman, 1995/6, p.47.

Thomas Gainsborough
(1727-1788), *Portrait of a
Gentleman*, 1743-1744,
Graphite on vellum,
12.2 x 10.9 cm
Photo © National Gallery of
Ireland

Suffolk Fund which was raised in 1745 to oppose the Young Pretender includes subscriptions from the artist's cousins John Gainsborough for £25, and from Elizabeth Gainsborough for 10 guineas.

Thickness implies that the courtship was brief, the meeting and marriage taking place 'when he obtained his nineteenth year'. How he met his future wife is told in a much later account: it was through Margaret's brother who was employed by Gainsborough's father 'as a travelling agent to assist him in his mercantile pursuits'.[92] Fulcher's account went on to describe Gainsborough drawing a landscape when Margaret Burr inadvertently drifted in, to be captured by the artist. There is also a sketch of Margaret Burr that was described earlier by Thornbury: 'I have now a sketch of himself and his wife on a small piece of paper before they were married. She was very pretty. They are both strong likenesses, as I was told by a sister of my father's who knew them'.[93]

death on 24 February 1745 meant that the annuity was known about, and possibly payments had begun by the time of her marriage to Gainsborough in July 1746.

Thickness described Margaret Burr as 'a very pretty Scots girl, of low birth'. This is a clear reference to her descent; her mother Margaret Aikman married her father William Burr in Edinburgh around 1718. It is uncertain what elicited Margaret senior's move from Scotland to London although it may have been the death of her husband, where she met Henry Somerset. Somerset was a well-known Jacobite, although he died just months before the 'Young Pretender,' Prince Charles Edward, landed on Eriskay Island and began the Forty-Five Rebellion. He also missed, unlike Gainsborough's young artist friends and possibly Gainsborough himself, the execution of the Jacobite Lords at Tower Hill in the aftermath of the rebellion.[91] The dissenting Gainsborough family were certainly opposed to the Jacobites, and the

It is probable that by the time they met, Margaret was a very eligible young woman and that Gainsborough was set up in the City of London in Little Kirby Street, just off Hatton Garden.[94] Edwards had noted that 'After quitting his master [Hayman], he for some time resided in Hatton-garden, and practised painting of portraits of a small size, and also pursued his favourite subject: landscape'.[95] This fits in with a mid-nineteenth-century account that stated, like Edwards, 'He also became a pupil of Hayman, but after a short and unprofitable residence with him he hired a room with a Mr. Jorden'.[96] Jorden, was, like Gainsborough's brother Humphrey, training for the ministry and became the Reverend John Jorden around December 1746. Hatton Garden was in the parish of St Andrews Holborn and it appears that Gainsborough was part of the congregation of that Church. Two early portraits now in the National Gallery of Ireland illustrate the manner of portraits that he was engaged upon at this time, around 1743 and 1734, at the age of 16 or 17.

(Detail of)
Thomas Gainsborough
(1727-1788), *Portrait of
the Artist with his Wife
and Daughter*, about
1748, Oil on canvas,
92.1 x 70.5 cm
© The National Gallery,
London. Acquired under
the Acceptance-in-lieu
scheme at the wish of
Sybil, Marchioness of
Cholmondeley, in
memory of her brother,
Sir Philip Sassoon,
1994.

[91] John Taylor, pupil of Hayman, amongst an enormous crowd recalled seeing the rebel lords executed at Tower Hill on 18 August 1746, see *Gentleman's Magazine,* 1839, p.100.

[92] Fulcher, 1856, p.4.

[93] Rev. Kirby Trimmer quoted in Thornbury, 1862, vol.2, p.59.

[94] David Tyler, 'Thomas Gainsborough's days in Hatton Garden,' *Gainsborough's House Review*, 1992/3, pp.27–32.

[95] Edwards, 1808, p.130.

[96] J. M. [probably John Mitford, d.1859] editor of the *Gentleman's Magazine*, 1856 review of Fulcher, p.199,

[97] John Southerden Burn, *The History of the Fleet Marriages*, London, 1846.

It is difficult to know how speedy the courtship between Thomas and Margaret was, but know that the marriage itself was quite speedy because it was what was known as a 'Fleet marriage'.[97] This was a marriage that was quick, legal and could take place without any public knowledge. The decision of Thomas and Margaret to marry at the Chapel was either for speed, to be clandestine, or both. What is uncertain is the reason for this. The main reasons for embarking on such a marriage were early pregnancy, incompatibility of age or religion or family objections. In the Gainsboroughs' case age was not an issue, being both over the legal age to marry, both having been born in 1727. The most likely and accepted speculation, though we cannot be certain, is that Margaret was pregnant.

Thomas Gainsborough married Margaret Burr on 15 July 1746 at the 'little New Chapel, in May Fair', near Hyde Park Corner. Costing a guinea for a legal marriage, it included the Clerk and Minister's fees and a certificate. Known as Mr Keith's Chapel, the building, where the Minister and Clerk also lived, was within ten yards of St George's Chapel, Curzon Street, where Keith had been Minister. Alexander Keith (d.1758) had been excommunicated on 27 October 1742 and committed to Fleet Prison in 1743 where he continued to run his marriage business, initially at the prison and then through staff at his New Chapel Mayfair, where Thomas Gainsborough married. Hardly surprisingly, the Fleet prison was less attractive to couples than Mr Keith's New Chapel which boasted a 'Porch at the Door like a Country Porch Door'.[98]

Advertising that it was 'to prevent mistakes,' it was a hasty and easy way to be legally married, not requiring banns to be read on three successive Sundays, with all publicity or objections conveniently avoided. It was very lucrative for Keith who from setting up in 1735 to his excommunication raised the number of marriages from single figures to 723 in 1742. This incurred the wrath of Dr Trebeck, rector of

Thomas Gainsborough (1727-1788), *Anne Lynch*, c.1744, Pencil on vellum, 12x10 cm © Gainsborough's House, Sudbury, Suffolk

the adjacent church of St George's, Hanover Square, Margaret Burr's parish church, whose weddings had decreased by over a third in this period, and who prosecuted Keith's excommunication. The marriages performed at the chapel remained legal until the Marriage Act of 1753, which came into operation on 25 March 1754. On 24 March that year 61 couples married at Mr Keith's Little Chapel.

Gainsborough's accommodation at Little Kirby Street was modest and although it suited Gainsborough at this time, it was unsuitable for a married man with the possibility of beginning a family. A house was found around the corner at Hatton Garden, where Gainsborough continued his painting practise asking 'the 3 to 5 gns. [for a portrait] he is said to have charged when he set up with Margaret Burr in Hatton Garden.'[99] In March 1746/47 Gainsborough's name appears in the rate book for Hatton Garden. Much later the artist recalled his early life: 'I don't think I am a bit altered since I lived in Hatton Garden only that I'm grey in the Poll – my Wife says I am not so good as I was then tho I take more pains'.[100]

[98] *The General Advertiser*, 20 July 1744.
[99] John Bensusan-Butt, *Burlington Magazine*, July 1985, p.459.
[100] Thomas Gainsborough to James Unwin 25 May 1768, in Hayes, 2001, no.31.

Jacobus Houbraken (1698-1780), by Hubert-François Gravelot (né Bourguignon (1699-1773)), *George Frideric Handel*, 1738, from 'The Heads of Illustrious Persons in Great Britain', 1743, Line Engraving, 360 mm x 225 mm © National Portrait Gallery, London Handel, who dominated the musical world, was a fellow member of the congregation at the same church as Margaret Burr, Gainsborough's wife-to-be.

Thomas Gainsborough (1727-88), *Study of a young woman (possibly Margaret Burr)*, c. 1746-48, Black chalk, 35.3 x 32.6 cm, RCIN 931554 (verso)
Royal Collection Trust / © Her Majesty Queen Elizabeth II 2018
Newly discovered sketch on the reverse of a landscape drawing, which may be Margaret Gainsborough at the moment when the artist first saw his future wife as described by Fulcher. (see p.69)

It is difficult to know when the Gainsboroughs' first child was born and a Christening record is still to be found. Certainly there is no record of baptism in St Andrews, Holborn, which was their church. The only thing we really know is that their daughter, 'Mary Gainsborough of Hatton Garden,' was buried at St Andrews on 1 March 1747/48. There is twenty months between their marriage and the death of their first child and the age of their daughter could have been anything from death at birth up to around eighteen months old. If the first Mary Gainsborough is memorialised in the charming portrait of Thomas, Margaret and daughter (National Gallery), it dates the scene to around 1747/48. Although no text is legible in the paper in Gainsborough's hand, one is tempted to think that it might depict the certificate from Mr Keith's chapel.

1748 was a pivotal year for Gainsborough: on the one hand the year brought personal tragedy, with the newly married artist burying his first child in March and his father in October. These events were tied up with his growing professional reputation. With his training complete, he made the decision to return to Suffolk. His professional success in this difficult year saw his joining the burgeoning British art world at the Foundling Hospital alongside his first mention in print in the November's *Universal Magazine* within a group of artists: 'who have distinguished themselves by their performances ... who are justly esteemed eminent masters.'[101]

The Foundling Hospital, a charity founded by the philanthropic sea captain Thomas Coram (c. 1668–1751), in 1739, first opened its doors to children in Hatton Garden in 1741. The newly purpose-built hospital, at Lamb's Conduit Fields, began to receive children on four years later in 1745. Coram was a dominant figure and a pillar of the church at St Andrew's Holborn, the same church to which Thomas and Margaret Gainsborough belonged. He must have been aware of Gainsborough and the burial of their

Thomas Gainsborough (1727-1788), *A Boy with a Book and Spade*, 1748, Pencil on paper, 189 x 153 mm
© The Morgan Library & Museum

Thomas Gainsborough (1727-1788), *The Charterhouse*, 1748, Oil on canvas, 55.8 x 55.8 cm
© Coram in the care of the Foundling Museum

A View of the Foundling Hospital

B. Cole, *A View of the Foundling Hospital*, c 1750, Etching
© Gainsborough's House, Sudbury, Suffolk

W. Hogarth inv. et delin.   *L. Sullivan Sculp.*

Whoever makes a DESIGN *without the Knowledge of* PERSPECTIVE *will be liable to such Absurdities as are shewn in this* Frontispiece.

William Hogarth (1697 - 1774) Frontispiece etching with engraving in Joshua Kirby's *Dr Brook Taylor's Method of Perspective made easy; Both in Theory and Practice:...,* Published London, 1768 © Gainsborough's House, Sudbury, Suffolk

The Charter House Hospital

Toms *Sc.*

Toms, *The Charter House Hospital*, c 1750, Etching
© Gainsborough's House, Sudbury, Suffolk
The red dot marks the viewpoint of Gainsborough's Charterhouse

child in March that year, and possibly furthered the commission of Gainsborough to paint one of London's hospitals for the Court Room. Gainsborough appears to be the last artist to be asked and certainly the youngest (at the age of 21). This was undoubtedly prestigious for the artist as the Foundling Hospital had become, through Hogarth, a prominent public venue for the exhibition of new British art.

As Edwards recalled:

> The present building [the Foundling Hospital] was erected; but as the income of the charity could, with no propriety, be expended upon decorations, many of the principal artists of that day voluntarily exerted their talents for the purpose of ornamenting several of the apartments of the Hospital, which otherwise must have remained without decoration. The pictures thus produced, and generously given, were permitted to be seen by any visitor, upon proper application. The spectacle was so new, that it made a considerable impression upon the public, and the favourable reception these works experienced, impressed the artists with an idea of forming a public Exhibition, which scheme was carried into full effect in the following manner.[102]

For the Foundling Hospital Gainsborough produced a painting that is a masterclass in topographical perspective, *The Charterhouse*, 1748 (Foundling Museum). This was painted as one of eight roundels representing London hospitals for the Court Room of the Foundling Hospital. These were painted by the leading British landscape painters: Samuel Wale (1721?–1786), who became the first Professor of Perspective at the Royal Academy on 17 December 1768, Edward Haytley (*fl.* 1740–1764), Richard Wilson (1712/13–1782), and the final one by Gainsborough, the youngest of the painters. Gainsborough's painting,

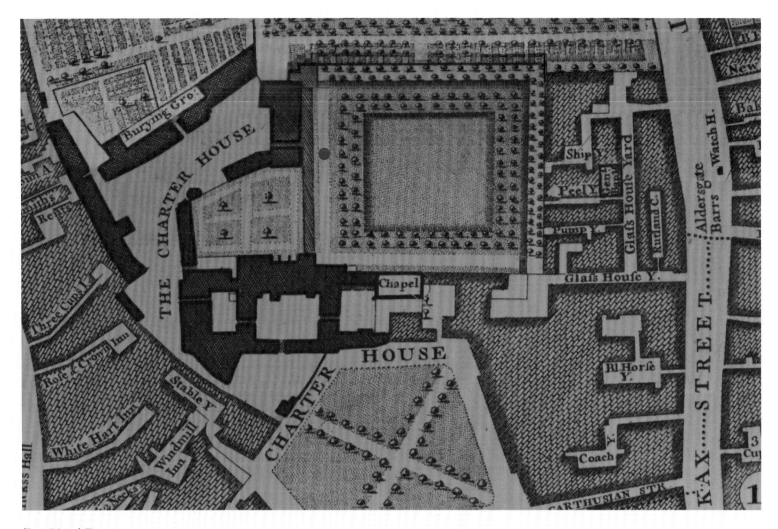

(Detail from) The Charterhouse from *A Plan of the Cities of London and Westminster, and Borough of Southwark*, surveyed by John Rocque and engraved by John Pine, 1746, Paper, 700 x 503 mm (indiv. plate)
© The Trustees of the British Museum
The red dot marks the viewpoint of Gainsborough's *Charterhouse*

a 'view of *Sutton's* hospital, called the Charter House,' as it was described in the eighteenth century, depicts the cloister terrace looking towards the Bowling Green and Chapel Tower.[103] If we compare it to John Roque's 1746 map of London, we can clearly see the point from which Gainsborough took the view.[104] The position is head height and looks directly south, with a single vanishing point, one third in and up from the right, falling at the door that viewer is directly facing. The light is coming from the west, and it is sunset by the evocation of still light, which seventeenth-century Dutch painters so revelled in. The severity of such simple perspective is softened by the sophistication of the painting.

It is interesting to compare this roundel of *The Charterhouse* for the Foundling Hospital with the other (older) landscape painters who contributed pieces. George Vertue (1684–1756) highlighted the painting in August 1751, writing, '… in the foundling Hospital in the Governors Room where the pictures are. Is small rounds prospects & views of the Several Hospitals – very well done. Amongst them those done by. Gainsboro – are tho't the best & masterly manner…'.[105] One of the characteristics that distinguished Gainsborough from the other artists was his masterly technique, which is associated with Dutch seventeenth-century landscape painting. The painting, for example, as Rica Jones has demonstrated in *The Making of*

---

[101] *The Universal Magazine*, November 1748, p.232.

[102] Edwards, 1808, p.xxiv.

[103] Sir Thomas Bernard, *An Account of the Hospital for the Maintenance and Education of Exposed and Deserted Young Children*, London, 1796, p.20.

[104] *A plan of the cities of London and Westminster, and borough of Southwark*, surveyed by John Rocque and engraved by John Pine, 1746.

[105] George Vertue Notebooks, 1933-34, Vertue III, p.157.

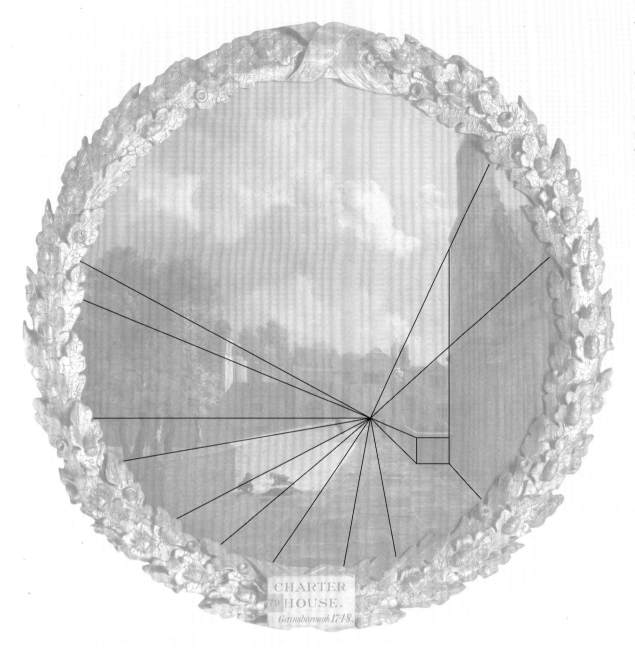

Thomas Gainsborough
(1727-1788), *The Charterhouse,* 1748, Oil on canvas, 55.8 x 55.8 cm
© Coram in the care of the Foundling Museum
Gainsborough uses single point perspective for the composition of his painting.

CHARTER 79 HOUSE.
Gainsborough 1748.

Gainsborough's Early Landscapes deliberately uses an orange coloured ground rather than a pale grey ground, which helps it stand out from the others. This demonstrates how well Gainsborough had managed to adopt the excellence of the Dutch method.

In 1772, the *Town and Country Magazine* recalled that, 'Whether from disgust, or from other motives, I know not; but he retired some where in the country, in Essex or Suffolk'.[106] It is unlikely that the move was as final as the gossipy magazine suggests and there is little doubt that Gainsborough made the journey between London and Sudbury throughout the year.

There was a regular coach service, and the subjects of his paintings of the 1740s, of London and Sudbury, indicate his presence in both places throughout the decade, 1748 in particular. *The Charterhouse* was not the only masterpiece that Gainsborough painted in this year, and his *Cornard Wood* according to the artist himself 'was actually painted at Sudbury, in the year 1748'.[107] An intriguing Gainsborough receipt in Gainsborough's House dating from 1759 suggests that he was also staying in London from time to time, in this case at Hatton Garden after his move back to Suffolk.

On 29 August of the same year the Reverend Stephen White opened a village school at Holton St Mary, Suffolk, some 14 miles from Sudbury. It was announced by a sign 'Not Slothful in Business Serving the Lord.' At the centre of the sign is a figure of a youth, with a spade in one hand representing diligent work and a book in the other representing study. Sadly the sign today is quite damaged, but the original drawing for the sign, all squared up with its design ready to be transferred to the sign, is by Gainsborough and is now in the Pierpoint Morgan Library, New York.

The move back to Sudbury and the surrounding towns and villages of Suffolk was not such an onerous transition. Here his daughters were born and Christened and his business as a painter continued rather than started afresh.

[106] Anon., 1772, p.486.
[107] Thomas Gainsborough to Henry Bate Dudley 11 March 1788, in Hayes, 2001, No.104.

(Detail of)
Thomas Gainsborough
(1727-1788), *Peter
Darnell Muilman,
Charles Crokatt and
William Keable in a
Landscape*, c.1750,
Oil on canvas,
76.3 x 63.5 cm
© Gainsborough's
House, Sudbury, Suffolk
and Tate, London 2018

'RETURNED TO HIS NATIVE TOWN'

The date of the return to his hometown of Sudbury with his wife is uncertain, It was either late 1748 or early 1749. We know from his paintings that in the 1740s he travelled and worked in both London and Suffolk. Hayman's letter from around 1746 where he sought to commission Gainsborough 'whilst he is in Town'[108] also confirms this. There is no reason to suppose that he did not continue to visit regularly and to stay in London after 1749. According to Fulcher, a Sudbury man, his return was due to circumstances: 'Sitters were few; dealers proved poor paymasters; and clay figures yielded but little sustenance. He therefore determined to leave London; and packing up canvas and colours returned to his native town ...'.[109] His residence according to Fulcher was 'in comfortable circumstances ... in Friars' Street', the street on which he had been baptised. Gainsborough's name appears independently in the Sudbury rate books from the

Spring of 1749, though the exact location of his residence is debated.[110]

Gainsborough returned to a Sudbury that had suffered from a smallpox epidemic. All Saints Church, where Mr Andrew married Miss Carter on 10 November 1748, had witnessed over 80 burials in a year.[111] Despite this, Thomas and Margaret started a new family with the birth of their second daughter Mary, who was Christened at All Saints on 3 February, 1750 and their third daughter Margaret who was Christened at St Gregory's, Sudbury, on 22 August 1751. It is interesting to note that the daughters were Christened in Anglican Churches rather than having a Dissenting baptism, and that this occurred at different churches in Sudbury. This may indicate a change in address, or else that they wished to be involved with both the churches strongly associated with the Gainsborough family.

Thomas Gainsborough (1727-1788), *Mr and Mrs Andrews*, about 1750, Oil on canvas, 69.8 x 119.4 cm
© The National Gallery, London. Bought with contributions from The Pilgrim Trust, The Art Fund, Associated Television Ltd, and Mrs and Mrs. W. W. Spooner, 1960.

Thomas Gainsborough
(1727-1788), *Mr & Mrs John Browne and their daughter, Anna Maria,* c. 1754-55,
Oil on Canvas, 80 x 104 cm
© Private Collection
Norfolk UK

Thomas Gainsborough (1727-1788), *Thomas Gainsborough,*
c. 1759, Oil on canvas
© National Portrait Gallery, London

Thomas Gainsborough (1727-1788), *Margaret Gainsborough (1728-1798),* 1758, Oil on canvas,
76 x 63.5cm
© bpk / Gemäldegalerie, SMB / Volker-H. Schneider

Thomas Gainsborough (1727-1788), *Peter Darnell Muilman, Charles Crokatt and William Keable in a Landscape,* c.1750, Oil on canvas, 76.3 x 63.5 cm
© Gainsborough's House, Sudbury, Suffolk and Tate, London 2018

Gainsborough was already established as a painter in the region, with paintings for Suffolk clients of both landscapes and portraits throughout the 1740s. Amongst the most influential of his Sudbury clients were the Carter family, which has been mentioned earlier. In this period Gainsborough developed the conversation piece to a whole new level as his portraiture developed to a sophistication that matched his landscape painting. Gainsborough had already achieved a masterpiece of landscape painting in Sudbury in 1748 with *Cornard Wood*, 1748 (National Gallery, London) before 1750 around which time he painted *Mr and Mrs Andrews*, c.1750 (National Gallery, London) and *Muilman, Crockatt and Keable in a Landscape*, c.1750 (Gainsborough's House/Tate). These conversation pieces, particularly *Mr and Mrs Andrews*, have reached iconic status within British art at the apex of the *genre*, but as such, somewhat divorced from their original context. *Mr and Mrs Andrews* is one of the greatest achievements of this period and of the *genre*, with landscape and the portrait as intimately and brilliantly connected as its sitters are with their ownership. She is Miss Carter of the family whose Gainsborough's father was in debt to when he died in 1748. Mrs Andrews' lap is enigmatically unfinished. The reason for this omission is uncertain, and speculations have ranged from seeing it as a place to add a future child to theories of sexual innuendo. The presence of light sketching and a feather indicate that it was likely to have been a game bird, possibly with the intention to paint it, as Rica Jones has suggested, when Mr Andrews had at last succeeded in shooting one.

Gainsborough's move away from the conversation piece began in the early 1750s, when there was created a greater dichotomy between his landscape and portrait painting. Changes in artistic fashion, the demands of the sitter as well as his own development as a painter contributed this move. Despite this there are further great examples of 'pictures in little,' from the early 1750s including *Mr & Mrs John Browne and their daughter, Anna Maria*, c.1754–55 at Houghton Hall.

Given his background, training, and his restless energy, Gainsborough as an artist continued to explore new forms in his art. He had soaked up the influence of his boyhood in Sudbury, not just by imitating the paintings and drawings that captivated him: the landscape that surrounded him remained something of an ideal in his mind's eye. In London, the student had benefitted from training and mentoring with the artistic world. In Sudbury from 1748 he was in control of his medium, having reached a point where his paintings are the explorations of a master.

---

108 Quoted in Allen, 1987, p.92.
109 Fulcher, 1856, p.31.
110 Lindsay Stainton and Bendor Grosvenor, *Tom will be a Genius*, Philip Mould, London, 2009, p.28.
111 William Walter Hodson, *The Meeting House and the Manse*, London, 1893, pp.71–2.

THE MAKING OF GAINSBOROUGH'S EARLY LANDSCAPES

Rica Jones

In the early 1750s Gainsborough received a commission from 'a gentleman near Ipswich' to paint a group of gipsies in a landscape (fig.1).[1] Calling by one day when the painting was in progress, the gentleman near Ipswich said he did not like it, whereupon Gainsborough took up his palette knife and slashed the painting, saying 'Then you shall not have it'. This account comes to us indirectly from Mr Trimmer, the great-grandson of Gainsborough's close friend Joshua Kirby, who had begged the damaged *Landscape with Gipsies* from the artist and had it mended (fig.2). Although published more than seventy years after Gainsborough's death and with its accuracy questionable in some areas, Trimmer's account is interesting nevertheless for some of its observations on Gainsborough's methods of painting - as well as giving us a striking glimpse of the artist's mercurial temperament.[2]

Referring again to the *Landscape with Gipsies*, Trimmer stated, '… Gainsborough in his early works, owing to his great execution, finished as he went on …'.[3] This means that he finished the different parts of the composition one after another, rather than moving from area to area in a more studied fashion to keep the whole painting at a consistent balance. Looking at the painting, we can see that this is true: the sky, the central tree and the figures are well on the way to being finished. Perhaps Gainsborough was working on these areas when the gentleman near Ipswich came to call. On the unfinished far left side of the picture, however, we see that a certain amount of planning had taken place at an earlier stage; the artist had established the bare bones of the composition with very sketchy oil paint, applied in a broad linear fashion; in this area we can make out a small pond

with a hillock beyond it and a goat standing half way up. Like all the paintings from these early years, *Landscape with Gipsies* displays within its small format the whole range of features for which Gainsborough's work from later periods has been valued: the light touch, elegant forms, glowing colours, subtle tones, varied surfaces and inspired brushwork. Although his style changed as the decades passed, the fundamental techniques that underpinned it remained the same. Before looking at those techniques in detail, it would be helpful to look briefly at the artistic scene that Gainsborough entered in London as a boy in his thirteenth year.

In the seventeenth century the general practice was to paint most of the composition in solid, opaque colours followed by highlights and glazing with translucent paint to enrich or deepen them. Although this could be abbreviated to suit the painter's individual style, it remained the principal way of producing a picture, especially in portraiture. The practice continued into the eighteenth century but became considerably reduced or was replaced by other methods. London in the 1740s was a fertile place to be an artist, with freedom to develop as an individual. As discussed later in this essay, colourshops existed to supply all materials ready prepared; and that traditional moderator of standards, the guild of painting, had dwindled to the point of irrelevance. The Company of Painter-Stainers of London appears never to have enjoyed the power of guilds on the continent of Europe, Antwerp's for example. Its history is one of litigation against other companies such as the Plasterers, whose members strayed over into painters' territory.[4] One of the Painter-Stainers' prerogatives was the impromptu search of artists' premises in the City of London and

---

[1] Walter Thornbury, *The Life and Correspondence of J.M.W. Turner, R.A.,* 2nd edition, 1877, reprinted Ward Lock, 1970, p.247. Mr. Trimmer communicated his information direct to Walter Thornbury. *Landscape with Gipsies* dates from not later than September 1755, when Joshua Kirby left Ipswich for London. (see Felicity Owen, 'Joshua Kirby', *Oxford Dictionary of the National Biography,* http://www.oxforddnb.com/articles/15/15646, 19.7.2017.

[2] An example of questionable accuracy is Trimmer's assertion that Gainsborough used wax in his early work (Thornbury 1877, p.251). To date, this material has not been found by materials analysis of Gainsborough's paintings.

[3] Thornbury 1862, p. 247. It is interesting to note that later on Gainsborough altered this approach and worked up the whole painting as he progressed. In his 14th discourse, Sir Joshua Reynolds praises Gainsborough for, '…his manner of forming all the parts of his picture together: the whole going on at the same time …'. See Robert E. Wark (ed.), *Discourses on Art: Sir Joshua Reynolds,* London and New York, p.221.

within a four-mile compass around it, in order to check on such things as the treatment of apprentices and indeed to ensure that apprentices were properly indentured. The last recorded search outside of the City of London was in 1708, after which the company regulated only the trades of painting.[5] With the reduction of regulation came the freedom to set up as a painter without formal training, Hogarth a prime example, and in the portraiture of the 1740s we see individual styles of painting underpinned by equally individual techniques, the latter an unusual

development.[6] It must have been a most stimulating place to be a young painter, and we can be sure that Gainsborough looked around him avidly to take note of what could be done with paint.

Gainsborough's paintings are almost all on plainly woven, linen canvas of medium weight.[7] Most British painters in the 1740s used this type of support. In his grounds, however, Gainsborough soon displayed his independence of his contemporaries in the London art world, a move that tells us that the colour of the

Fig.1
Thomas Gainsborough
(1727-1788), *Landscape with Gipsies*, c.1753-4, Oil paint on canvas, ©Tate, London 2018

[4] See W. A. D. Englefield, *The History of the Painter-Stainers Company of London*, London, 1923 (reprinted 1950), *passim*.
[5] Englefield 1923, p.161.
[6] See Rica Jones, 'The Artist's Training and Techniques', in Elizabeth Einberg (ed.), *Manners and Morals: Hogarth and British Painting* 1700–1760, exhibition catalogue, London, 1987, pp.24–27.

Fig.2

Landscape with Gipsies photographed in raking light from the left to show the marks of the slashes made by Gainsborough.

ground was important to him.[8] Many of the early paintings are on pale grey or greyish fawn coloured grounds.[9] In this Gainsborough was following a tradition that was probably established in London by Sir Godfrey Kneller, the German-born painter who became the leading Baroque portraitist in Britain from around 1680 until his death in 1723.[10] Most of the painters associated with the second St Martin's Lane Academy in the 1740s used grey grounds,[11] and through his early mentors, Hubert Gravelot and Francis Hayman, Gainsborough had some acquaintance with this evening academy, which had

---

[7] The thread count of Gainsborough's paintings varies from 15 to 18 picks horizontally and vertically per square centimetre. Hayes records one early painting on wooden panel and another on paper now laid onto canvas: see John Hayes, *The Landscape Paintings of Thomas Gainsborough*, London, 1982, vol.2, pp.355 and 377.

[8] The ground is a surface on which to paint; it is usually made from lean, opaque paint applied as a single, unmodified colour to the support in readiness for painting. For Gainsborough's grounds, see Rica Jones, 'Gainsborough's Methods and Materials: A 'remarkable ability to make paint sparkle'', Young Gainsborough, London, 1997, pp.19–21.

[9] See Rica Jones, Fragment Portraits, pp 102–104.

[10] Jones, 1987, pp.24–27.

[11] See Jones, 1987, pp.20–22.

been established in 1735 by William Hogarth for drawing and painting from the life. These grounds are made of lean, greyish paint containing lead white, chalk (calcium carbonate) and varying amounts of black and earth colours all bound together in linseed oil.[12] Gainsborough's paint being rather thin on the whole, the underlying colour of the ground greatly informs the overall tonality of the painting even when it is not itself left visible as a colour in its own right. Mostly, though, Gainsborough did allow the ground's colour to stand here and there within the composition, as in Figure 3, where the grey ground is left visible at the edges of the clouds to help define them. Another feature of these grounds is that their surface is minutely striated with grooves, usually two or three to a millimetre's width (fig.4).[13] This finely grooved texture must have lent purchase to Gainsborough's swiftly moving brush. The striations are always consistently horizontal or vertical throughout the painting, and they relate to the tool with which the ground was applied to the bare canvas. Once again they are found commonly in British paintings from the 1730s to the 1750s, and in many instances they indicate manufacture by artists' colourmen, who were much used by painters in London in this period. We know that by the 1740s

there existed in the capital city many colourshops and at least one that catered specifically for artists rather than painters and decorators.[14] In this period no artist in London had to prime his own canvases or grind his own paint unless he wished to.

By 1748, however, Gainsborough had departed from contemporary practice by choosing to paint some of his work on orange coloured grounds.[15] None of his contemporaries in London are known to have used this ground colour. The first securely datable of Gainsborough's is *The Charterhouse* (fig.5, p.74), which was presented by the artist to the Foundling Hospital (now the Foundling Museum) in May 1748.[16] The painting is one of a set of roundels in the Courtroom depicting hospitals in London; two are by Richard Wilson, three by Samuel Wale and two by Edward Haytley. The whole decorative scheme for the Courtroom was almost certainly orchestrated by Hogarth, a friend of the founder, Thomas Coram. As Mark Bills has discussed in *'From the obscurity of a Country Town; …* (pp.72–76), these painters were all older than Gainsborough and all were well established in London. The canvas for their seven roundels was cut from the same long piece, and they all have the same pale grey grounds.[17] Although the stretcher of

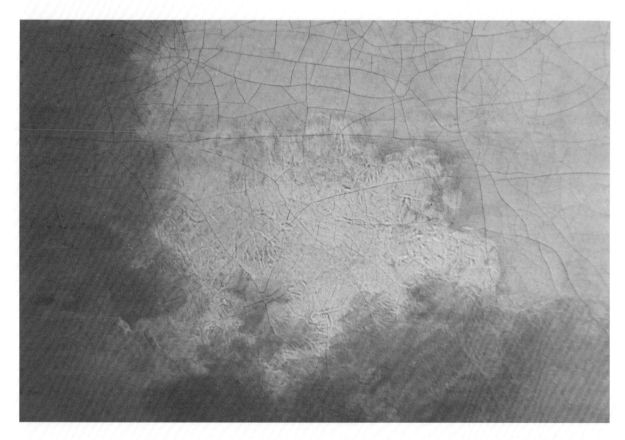

Fig.3
Detail of the sky of *Wooded Landscape with a Herdsman Resting*, showing the grey ground peeping through at the edge of the pink cloud.

Fig.4
Detail of *Wooded Landscape with a Herdsman Resting*, (see pp.54–55) in raking light from the top right, showing the horizontal, ridged striations in the ground and soft impasto in the foliage.

Gainsborough's painting is the same as all of the others, his canvas is slightly finer and there is no trace of a grey ground underneath the orange colour. Was Gainsborough perhaps in Sudbury when he did this work or, at twenty years of age, was he sufficiently sure of his technical needs that he could insist on his own terms? The evidence of the stretcher suggests the latter. We can be certain, however, that the effect of the orange ground was not lost on Hogarth. In this author's study of Hogarth's work, his grounds are darkish grey or fawn – except one, *O the Roast Beef of Old England ('The Gate of Calais')* (fig.6), which has an

---

[12] See Jones, 1987, p.24.

[13] Among 35 paintings by Gainsborough examined by the author, and dating from 1745 to about 1754, only two have grounds that are without striations. Forthcoming publication by Rica Jones.

[14] William T. Whitley, *Artists and their Friends in England 1700–1799*, London, 1928, vol.1, pp.330–333.

[15] The first published reference to the orange ground of *The Charterhouse* is in Viola Pemberton-Pigott, 'The Development of the Portrait of Countess Howe', *Earl and Countess Howe by Gainsborough*, Ed. Anne French, English Heritage, London, 1988, p.43.

[16] Hayes, 1982 vol.2. p.352. There are probably earlier examples, for example, *Woodland Landscape with Cottage*, Private Collection, formerly with Angus Neill of Felder Fine Art.

Fig.5
Detail of the tree on the
left of *The Charterhouse*,
showing the orange
coloured ground left visible
deliberately through the
branches and leaves.

Fig.6
William Hogarth
(1697-1764), *O, The Roast Beef
of Old England ('The Gate of
Calais')*, 1748. Oil on canvas,
78.8 x 94.5 cm
©Tate, London 2018

Fig.7

Close-up detail of the sky
and clouds of *The
Charterhouse*, showing
textured brushwork and
semi-translucent paint.

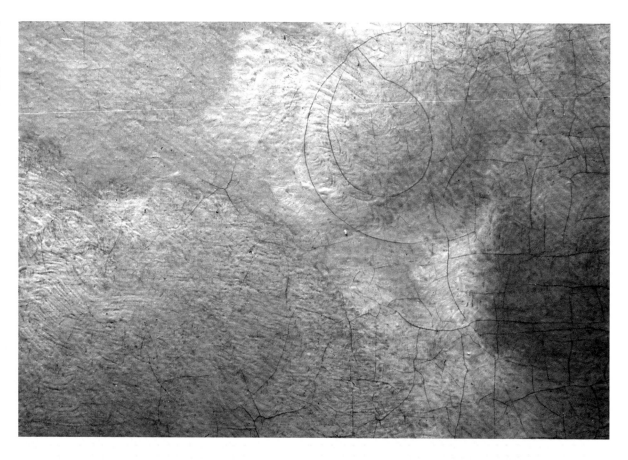

orange ground, very similar in tone to Gainsborough's.[18] Hogarth cannot have painted this picture earlier than *The Charterhouse* because it depicts his arrest at Calais while sketching the fortifications; travel from Britain to the continent of Europe was not feasible earlier than May 1748 on account of the War of the Austrian Succession.[19] Although Hogarth does not appear to have repeated the experiment, that orange ground is testament to how very impressed he was with Gainsborough's work in 1748. Gainsborough continued using grey, fawn or orange coloured grounds into the 1750s. After about 1755 a range of tan colours and russet pinks replaced those earlier colours. In Bath these reddish tones deepened sometimes to dark brick red.[20] In London Gainsborough's grounds became paler and cooler in tone.[21]

None of Gainsborough's paintings displays systematic drawing of the design on the primed canvas. Although some of his early landscape drawings are squared up, presumably for transfer of the design to another surface on a different scale, no equivalent drawn grid on a painting has been found to date. It should be noted, however, that if he drew gridlines on his primed canvases in chalk, that material would disappear underneath subsequent applications of paint.[22] For the bare bones of, his design, as we see in *Landscape with Gipsies,* he used brushed paint very sketchily. This early stage of painting was known then as the dead colouring, which was done either in monochrome oil paint or muted naturalistic tones made up of stable, inexpensive, low-key pigments such as the earth colours mixed with lead white.[23]

---

[17] Jones, 1997, p.20. See also Rica Jones and Martin Postle, 'Gainsborough in his Painting Room, in *Gainsborough*, exhibition catalogue, Tate Gallery, London, 2002, pp.29–30.

[18] Jones and Postle 2002, p.30.

[19] See Elizabeth Einberg and Judy Egerton, *The Age of Hogarth: British Painters Born* 1675–1709, Tate Gallery, London, 1988, pp.127–31. See also Jenny Uglow, *Hogarth: A Life and a World*, London 1997, p.461, 'In August [1748] … he set off for France with a group from St. Martin's Lane'.

[20] Pemberton-Pigott, 1988, p.41.

[21] Jones and Postle, 2002, p.37.

[22] Neither would it be detectable with infrared reflectography, which is used to render visible any underdrawing in carbon-based materials.

Fig.8
Detail of the right foreground of *Wooded Landscape with a Herdsman Resting* in slightly raking light from the right, showing staccato brushwork describing the grass.

Fig.9
Detail of brushwork in the foliage of *A Gentleman with a Dog in a Wood*, c.1746. Oil on canvas, private collection on loan to Gainsborough's House, Sudbury.

Fig.10
Thomas Gainsborough
(1727-1788), *Open
Landscape with Country
Wagon on an Undulating
Track,* 1746 - 1747
Oil on canvas, 48.3 x 60.3 cm
© Gainsborough's House,
Sudbury, Suffolk

The amount of dead colouring varied of course from artist to artist but, muted or monochrome, it was a standard feature of painting procedures of the period. It is rarely easily visible in Gainsborough's finished work, largely because he kept this stage of the process to a minimum.

It is interesting that, despite being so readily identifiable as Gainsborough's, no two of his early landscapes are quite the same in terms of the application of the paint. More than any other contemporary British painter of landscapes in the 1740s – Richard Wilson, George Lambert and John Wootton – Gainsborough revels in subtle texture – of his paint itself and of the landscape he is depicting. This called for specific brushwork and specific

materials. These little early landscapes all show delight in using the brush in different graphic ways with different thicknesses of paint to respond to nature's variety: the sky of *The Charterhouse* (fig.7), the distant foliage and the rough sedge in *Wooded Landscape with a Herdsman Resting* (figs 4 and 8), the detailed foliage of *A Gentleman with a Dog in a Wood* (fig.9), the rutted cart track in *Open Landscape with Country Wagon on an Undulating Track* (fig.10), the lichen on a branch in *Portrait of a Boy* (fig.11). So while it is true to say that Gainsborough, like most of his contemporaries, worked mainly in one layer of paint, applied wet-in-wet to the dead-coloured surface, it does not cover the subtlety of his observation and the inventiveness of his technique.[24] The grassy foreground of *Wooded Landscape with a Herdsman Resting*, for example, was

---

[23] Earth colours are known also as ochres. They are mainly red, yellow and brown clays, although nowadays they are often made synthetically.

[24] Wet-in-wet is the application of one colour next to or onto another, before the first has dried, so that some disturbance of the earlier application can occur.

Fig.11
Detail in slightly raking light from the right of lichen on a branch in *Portrait of a Boy (Fragment)*, c.1748. Oil on canvas, Gainsborough's House, Sudbury

oils needed thickening, which could be achieved either through heating the oil on its own or incorporating other substances such as resins; such oils were darker than the untreated ones and would become still darker with age. Specific analysis of an early self-portrait (see p.68) revealed heat-bodied linseed oil with added copal resin for the textured trunk of the tree behind the sitter.[26] Perhaps that is an instance of the gold-size that Mr Trimmer says Gainsborough used 'in the leafing of his trees'.[27] Gold size is used for applying gold leaf to surfaces when an oil-based adhesive is required. Made of oil made thick and sticky after heating with a resin and a drier, it would have produced the impasto that we see in some of Gainsborough's vegetation in this early period (fig.11). As well as rendering a painting-oil thicker and stiffer, the addition of a resin also makes it brighter and, at least when new, more translucent; those features would have appealed to Gainsborough but must have caused a certain amount of conflict in a man whose instinct was also to use stable materials that kept his paint looking bright.

Gainsborough used his pigments to their full capacity. All pigments provide colour but also bulk, texture and varying degrees of opacity and translucency. He favoured mainly the bright and translucent varieties from the range that was available to all painters and sometimes used them coarsely ground so as to produce large particles. Most British painters of this period used complex mixtures of pigments to produce a specific colour, but none more so than Gainsborough, to whom the correct tone was crucially important. The following pigments have all been found in his early work: translucent earth colours (siennas, umbers and Cologne earth); translucent bone black and opaque charcoal black: opaque red, yellow and orange earth colours; vermilion; translucent red, yellow, orange and brown lakes; Prussian blue, indigo blue and smalt (all translucent); blue verditer (opaque); Naples yellow and lead-tin yellow (both bright and opaque); orpiment (bright, semi-translucent and crusty); green earth (translucent); verdigris; lead white; powdered

painted a russet colour that was allowed to dry before the staccato strokes of thick yellow paint were applied to describe the rough sedge (fig.8).

In this period Gainsborough's chose his materials to produce bright colours, thixotropic paint (that is to say, paint that held the shape and texture of the brushstrokes without settling out or slumping), and above all translucency.[25] Analysis of his binding media in this period indicates that he respected tradition in substituting walnut and poppy oil for linseed in his whites, skies and a few other colours because when fresh those oils are less yellow than linseed, and may remain less yellow as they age. For texture, however,

---

[25] In later decades Gainsborough used thinner, more liquid paint, as attested by his daughter, who told Farington that unless her father held his palette horizontal, the paint on it would drip off the edge. Quoted in Helen Glanville, 'Gainsborough as Artist and Artisan', *A Nest of Nightingales*, Dulwich Picture Gallery, London, 1988, p.20 and note 62, p.26.

[26] Judy Egerton, *The British Paintings*, National Gallery, London, 1998, p.66.

[27] Thornbury, 1877, p.251.

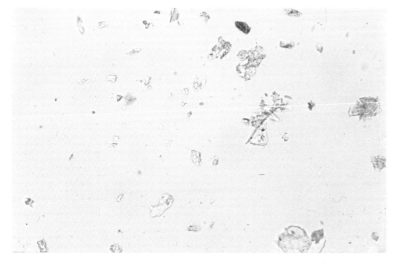

Fig.12

Green paint from *Lady Lloyd and Her Son, Richard Savage Lloyd, of Hintlesham Hall, Suffolk* (Yale Center for British Art, New Haven, Connecticut, USA, Paul Mellon Collection, B1981.25.293), photographed in transmitted polarised light at x400 magnification, showing ground glass, smalt, green earth, black and yellow lake pigments.

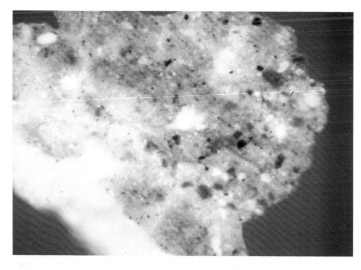

Fig.13

Tiny fragment of yellowish green paint from Gainsborough's *Rev John Chafy Playing the Violoncello in a Landscape,* c1750–52 (Tate T03895), photographed at x125 magnification to show the pigments. Photographed by Dr Ashok Roy at the National Gallery, London. The large number of different pigments in this sample (plus invisible ground glass) is typical of his work.

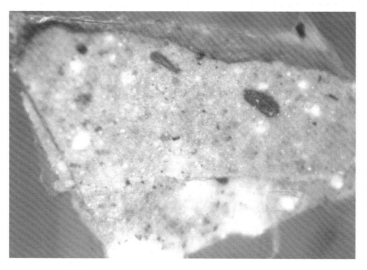

Fig.14

Tiny fragment of yellowish green paint from Francis Hayman's *The Wrestling Scene from 'As you like it',* c.1740–42 (Tate N06202), photographed at x125 magnification to show the pigments. Photographed by Dr Ashok Roy at the National Gallery, London.

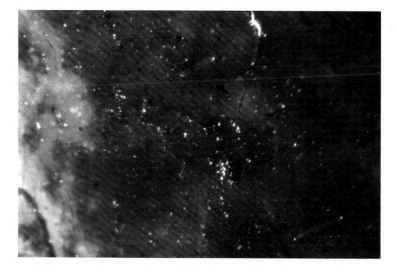

Fig.15

Red brick wall at the lower left edge of *The Charterhouse*, photographed at high magnification to show the orange ground on the extreme left, and translucent reddish brown paint.

Fig.16
Wooded Landscape with a Cottage and Shepherd
(Yale Center for British Art, New Haven, Connecticut, USA, Paul Mellon Collection, B1976.2.1).

chalk; ground glass.[28] The powdered chalk gave bulk when he wished to create soft texture without resorting to heat-treated oils. It is present in large quantities, for example, in the rounded, raised clumps of foliage in *Wooded Landscape with a Herdsman Resting* (see fig.4). Chalk, unlike lead white, becomes semi-translucent in oil and is therefore a useful bulking agent for a painter intent on creating paint that glows.

A consistent feature throughout his early period is the incorporation of glassy pigments in nearly all his colours. In many instances the glass is the blue pigment, smalt, which is blue glass ground down to a powder; in others, it appears to be just ground glass (fig.12). The purpose is at least two-fold: ground glass provides bulk to the paint without blocking light from reaching the range of pigments in any particular colour. This can be seen clearly in Figures 13 and 14: Figure 13 shows a tiny particle of an opaque yellowish green from the background of Gainsborough's *The Rev. John Chafy Playing the Violoncello in a Landscape* and Figure 14 is a similar green fragment from Francis

Hayman's *The Wrestling Scene from 'As you like it'*. It contains a similar range of pigments to Gainsborough's but with more lead white (which is opaque) and hardly any ground glass. As a result it looks dense and lacking in depth, unlike Gainsborough's glowing colours. In some paintings he went all-out for translucency: every colour in *The Charterhouse* contains smalt, even the brick reds of the buildings and the wall in the lower left corner. Figure 15 shows the very edge of that area, viewed at high magnification. The paint is translucent and glowing; light can reach the bright red particles of vermilion within the colour and also is reflected back from the underlying orange coloured ground.

Another reason for incorporating ground glass is that it helps the oil paint dry, while keeping it clear and unyellowed.[29] Many of the pigments that Gainsborough favoured – the lakes especially –- dry very slowly in oil without an agent to accelerate the process.[30] A more cynical explanation might be that ground glass is a cheap extender of paint, and as a

Fig.17
Detail of *Wooded Landscape with a Cottage and Shepherd*
The yellow highlights in the field are particles of orpiment.

[28] These pigments have been identified by the author with polarised light microscopy, followed by Energy-Dispersive X-ray analysis in a scanning electron microscope. The author is greatly indebted to Dr Joyce H. Townsend for operating the electron microscope and for her knowledge of pigments. For further information, see Jones, 'The Rev. John Chafy Playing the Violoncello in a Landscape', in Stephen Hackney, Rica Jones and Joyce Townsend (eds), *Paint and Purpose: a Study of Technique in British Art*, Tate Gallery, London, 1999, pp.48–53 and notes pp.203–4.

[29] See Marshall Smith, *The Art of Painting According to the Theory and Practice of the Best Italian, French and German Masters*, London, 1692, p.73.

young painter at the beginning of his career, Gainsborough might not have been able to afford expensive paint. It is possible – but in that case we might expect to find ground glass in similar quantities in the paint of at least some of his contemporaries, especially as some knowledge of using glassy pigments may have existed in London. Some of Kneller's paintings contain ground glass and this may have become known through his evening academy for painting and drawing from the life.[31] To date, however, it has not been found significantly in the work of Gainsborough's British contemporaries. One might expect glassy material used as a cheap filler in Hayman's work, as he had much experience of painting stage-sets for theatres, where extenders would be used in the paint to make it go further.[32] Yet Hayman's *See-Saw* (Tate T00524), one of the supper-box paintings for Vauxhall Gardens and therefore destined for a degree of wear-and-tear, does not contain significant quantities of glassy particles.[33] Other technical features that mark Gainsborough out among his British contemporaries are the choice of some pigments that by the 1740s were becoming old-fashioned, for example lead-tin yellow and verdigris; and, as we have discussed, large particle size, for example orpiment with particles so large they sit on the surface of the painting and catch the light (figs.16-17).

As few of these technical features appear significantly in the work of Gainsborough's British contemporaries, how did he come by them? Although we know he worked with Gravelot and Hayman and derived much graphic and stylistic knowledge from them both, the paint of neither matches Gainsborough's.[34] The use of glassy pigments as translucent fillers and dryers has a long history on the continent – especially in the Netherlands and in Italy.[35] It has been established that Gainsborough's early landscapes lean heavily stylistically on seventeenth-century Dutch works and, as Mark Bills has discussed (p.53), we know that Gainsborough added figures to Dutch seventeenth-century landscapes to increase their saleability. But day-to-day familiarity with seventeenth-century Dutch paintings cannot explain how Gainsborough knew about the use of glassy material; it cannot be seen in the paint with the unaided eye and therefore its use has to be taught directly by word, practice or both. Were there in London during the 1740s painters of Netherlandish origin who may have been involved in Gainsborough's early career? There is no documentation of such but the idea that Gainsborough had other instruction than has been documented goes back as far as his first biographer, Fulcher, who remarked that, 'Whatever knowledge he acquired of his art, beyond its elements, was gained from other instructors than Hayman and elsewhere than in the Academy in St. Martin's Lane.'[36] Further discussion of this question belongs elsewhere but suffice to say that analysis of paintings by likely contenders suggests that the Griffier family might fit the bill.[37] Jan Griffier the younger and Robert Griffier were both painting in London in the 1740s and via their father, Jan the Elder, came from a strong Netherlandish tradition. All the pigments found in Gainsborough's early landscapes occur in their work, including the use of glassy pigments.[38]

In Gainsborough's early landscapes, then, we find materials chosen specifically to produce bright colours, translucent paint, graphic descriptive

---

[30] Lake pigments are made from bright, translucent plant dyes, which are given body by being struck onto an inert, transparent material such as aluminium hydroxide.

[31] For Kneller's academy, see Whitley. 1928, pp.7–15. For the use of glassy material see Kneller, *Elijah and the Angel*, 1672, http://www.tate.org.uk/tudorandstuarttechnical research 4.7.2018.

[32] Brian Allen, *Francis Hayman*, Yale University Press, New Haven and London, 1987, pp.11–23.

[33] Analysis by R. Jones. For illustration of *See-Saw*, see Einberg and Egerton, 1988, p.41.

[34] Jones, 1997, p.25.

[35] See E. Melanie Gifford, 'A Technical Investigation of some Dutch Seventeenth-Century Tonal Landscapes', American Institute of Conservation Annual Meeting Preprints, Baltimore, 1983, pp.39–49. David Bomford, Christopher Brown and Ashok Roy, *Art in the Making: Rembrandt*, National Gallery, London, 1988, *passim*. Marika Spring, 'Colourless Powdered Glass as an Additive in Fifteenth- and Sixteenth-Century European Paintings', *National Gallery Technical Bulletin*, 2012, vol.33, pp.4–26.

[36] George Williams Fulcher, *Life of Thomas Gainsborough, R. A.*, London, 1856, p.29.

[37] This ongoing research will be the subject of a forthcoming paper by Rica Jones.

[38] Forthcoming paper, Rica Jones.

brushwork with subtle impasto, and a concern with long-term stability. Although his style developed over the decades, Gainsborough remained largely true to these technical principles. The coloured pigments listed above are found throughout his career, including chalk as a bulking agent.[39] Ground glass, on the other hand, is found much less as Gainsborough's paintings increased in size from the mid-to-late 1750s onwards; glassy paint would appear insubstantial in paintings of a larger scale. In later paintings we also find the expensive blue pigment, ultramarine, and in the 1780s the highly translucent Indian yellow, newly introduced from India.[40] Still concerned to use untreated oils for most of his work, as time went by Gainsborough appears to have used oleo-resinous paint more, although much less so than his contemporary, Sir Joshua Reynolds. *The Watering Place* of 1777 (National Gallery, London) appears to have oleo-resinous underlayers of paint, and in his last decade Gainsborough is said to have claimed that with asphaltum, 'he could have painted a pit as deep as the infernal regions'.[41] Asphaltum describes a range of tarry, bituminous substances that impart mellow translucency to dark colours when fresh but which are not always durable without cracking or darkening.[42] A number of paintings from Gainsborough's last decade show bad cracking that might be attributable to bituminous materials; that development would have pained him greatly had he lived to see it but, given the care he usually took to use durable materials, it shows us how fundamental was his preoccupation to create translucency in paint and make colours that were 'brilliant, sunny, harmonious'.[43]

Acknowledgements

The author would like to thank Dr Mark Hallett, Director of the Paul Mellon Centre for Studies in British Art, London; Mark Bills and his staff at Gainsborough's House, Sudbury, Suffolk; Dr Joyce Townsend of the Tate Gallery, London; Alexander Antrim, formerly Director of Conservation at the Tate Gallery; Karen Hearn, Julian Johns; Mia Jackson; Alice Tate-Harte; Victoria Sutcliffe, Dominic Tickell, Ellie Darton-Moore; all the owners of Gainsborough's early paintings who have allowed access to them.

Rica Jones

[39] See David Bomford, Ashok Roy and David Saunders, 'Gainsborough's 'Dr Ralph Schomberg'', *National Gallery Technical Bulletin*, 1988, vol.12, p.44.
[40] Forthcoming paper by Rica Jones for ultramarine; for Indian yellow, see Glanville, 1988, p.25.
[41] For *The Watering Place* see Egerton 1998, p.108. For asphaltum, see Jones and Postle, 2002, p.38, quoting *Art Union*, 1 September 1841, p.147.
[42] Leslie Carlyle, *The Artist's Assistant*, London, Archetype, 2001, pp.479–482.
[43] Fulcher 1856, p.177.

TWO FRAGMENT PORTRAITS BY THOMAS GAINSBOROUGH

Rica Jones

These paintings, which are fragments of a double portrait on a single canvas (figs 1–3), were acquired by Gainsborough's House respectively in 1984 and 1990.[1] In the past the portraits have been attributed by some scholars to Hogarth, by others to George Beare; and, although the fragments are now accepted as Gainsborough's by the majority of specialists in this area, the attribution is still debated by some. In 2017 the opportunity arose to do thorough technical examination of them and to compare the results with those from paintings known to be by Gainsborough in the 1740s and early 1750s.

Like all of Gainsborough's canvas paintings and most British paintings of the period, this double portrait is on plainly woven linen of medium weight.[2] The ground is pale, fawnish grey. As discussed in the essay *The Making of Gainsborough's Early Landscapes* (pp.87–88), most artists who were associated with the second St Martin's Lane Academy used grey grounds. In a study of 35 paintings done by Gainsborough before 1755, 32 are on canvas.[3] Of these 23 have fawnish grey grounds. Seven have orange grounds and one an initial grey ground with an opaque brownish pink priming on top of it. In *Landscape with Gypsies* the ground is closer to fawn. The *Self Portrait with Palette*, on card, also has a grey ground and two landscapes on recycled pine panels are painted over powder blue interior decorating paint (see the essay *Two Early Pastoral Landscapes*, p.113). The earliest datable orange ground is found in *The Charterhouse*, which Gainsborough presented to the Foundling Hospital in May 1748; but this is not to say that all grey grounds predate that year or that all orange grounds are post. *Mr and Mrs Andrews*, for example, has a grey ground but is most unlikely to have been painted before November 1748, the date of the Andrews' marriage.[4] It would appear that some time in the 1740s Gainsborough

---

[1] See Hugh Belsey, *Gainsborough at Gainsborough's House*, London, 2002, pp.15–16.
[2] The weave count of Gainsborough's early canvases varies from 12 to 18 picks per centimetre in both directions. This is standard for the period in British art.
[3] The author has spent many years collecting technical data on Gainsborough's early work, thanks mainly to the Tate Gallery, London, The Yale Center for British Art, New Haven and the Paul Mellon Centre for Studies in British Art, London.

Fig.1
Thomas Gainsborough (1727-1788), *Portrait of a Boy (Fragment of 'Portrait of a Boy and Girl')*, c.1744 Oil on canvas, 133.3 x 72.4 cm © Gainsborough's House, Sudbury, Suffolk

Fig.2
Thomas Gainsborough (1727-1788), *Portrait of a Girl (Fragment of 'Portrait of a Boy and Girl')*, c.1744, Oil on canvas, 44.8x33.5 cm
© Gainsborough's House, Sudbury, Suffolk

Fig.3
Diagram of the original format of the *Portrait of a Boy and Girl* From Hugh Belsey, *Gainsborough at Gainsborough's House,* London, 2002, p.15

started choosing his ground colour to suit the overall tonality of his projected composition, an interesting and unusual development in relation to his contemporaries in London.

Does the composition of the grey ground in the two fragment portraits resemble those of accepted paintings by Gainsborough? It does. They are all composed of lead white and chalk tinted with black and various earth pigments, all bound together in oil. Very often, like most British grounds of the period, they were applied in two or more coats, with what appears to be a coat of unpigmented animal glue size between them, as in this instance (fig.4). The proportion of chalk to lead white is high and the

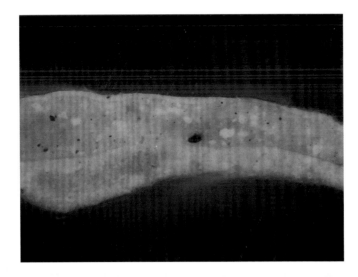

Fig.4
Cross-section sample from *Portrait of a Boy* in the area of the blue skirt, photographed at x200 magnification. Layered structure as shown in the diagram.

Thin, opaque pale blue paint of dress

Second coat of pale grey ground, probably darker than the first

Very thin coat of animal glue size

First coat of pale grey ground

Traces of animal glue size from the canvas

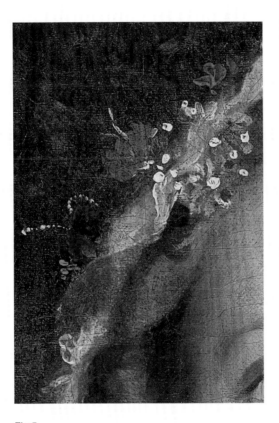

Fig.5
Detail of the girl's head, with horizontal striations in the ground beneath the paint.

Fig.6
Detail of the face in *Portrait of a Boy*.

Fig.7
Detail of the face of
Hogarth's *Mrs Salter*, 1741.
Oil on canvas
Tate N01663. © Tate, London
2018.

majority conform to general practice in having a
minutely striated surface (fig.5 – and fig.4 in the
essay *The Making of Gainsborough's Early Landscapes*,
p.89). But this type of construction is true also of
many paintings related to the second St Martin's
Lane Academy, including some of William
Hogarth's. As Hugh Belsey has noted, this double
portrait 'has a purity of colour and … a remarkable
ability to render the texture of fabrics which, as an
affirmation of quality, does much to explain the …
attribution to Hogarth'. Moreover, the technique
used in the faces of the children is Hogarthian.

Compare the face of the boy with Hogarth's *Mrs
Salter* of 1741 (figs 6–7). Both leave the underlying
grey ground visible to function as some of the half-
shadows, for example between the brow and the
hairline. Both display a brushy directness in the
application of the skin tones, hardly blended on the
canvas. What is different, however, is that Hogarth's
face has a full underpainting that is left visible to
form the recessive areas such as the eye sockets,
whereas Gainsborough's has no significant
underpainting.[5] We can make a similar comparison
with the technique used in the face of a portrait by

[4] National Gallery, London, NG6301. See Judy Egerton, *The British Paintings*, National Gallery, London, 1998, pp.80–87.
[5] Rica Jones, 'The Artists Methods and Materials', in Elizabeth Einberg, *Manners and Morals*, exhibition catalogue, Tate Britain, 1988, pp. 24–27.

George Beare (fig.8). The greyish skin tones visible at the temples, the eye sockets and the sides of the nose are what was then known as the dead colouring: the underpainting in cool, muted, naturalistic tones. The highlit areas were applied on top of this first phase after it had dried and they were blended together on the canvas. Apart from the line defining the sitter's left tearduct, no ground colour was left unpainted to form half-tones. The *Portrait of a Boy and Girl* was not painted by Hogarth or Beare; it was painted by a young artist who, as we know, would have seen Hogarth's work but not necessarily have had detailed knowledge of the techniques that underpinned it.

All the technical features analysed in these fragments conform to those found in accepted early works by Gainsborough. Close scrutiny of the painting reveals very faintly brushed drawing lines here and there, for example in the boy's left hand (fig.9). This may be compared to painted brown lines of drawing elsewhere, for example in figure 10, a detail from *Mrs Mary Cobbold with her Daughter Anne in a Landscape with a Lamb and Ewe* of c.1752. Mainly, though, the solid paint of the visible image covers any underdrawing. As discussed above, there appears to be no significant underpainting except very thin, sketchy brushwork here and there in the blue skirt; this is consistent in his work, as discussed in *The Making of Gainsborough's Early Landscapes* (pp.91–93). The paint that we see is mainly creamy in consistency and was applied directly with vigorous, descriptive brushwork. Gainsborough's characteristic method of painting volume as tonal shapes, the different tones largely unblended into one another on the canvas, can be seen throughout the painting, for example in Figure 11. In areas where nothing much is happening, the brush makes zig-zag marks, as in the near foreground (fig.12). This may be seen in a much smaller format in another very early painting, the *A Gentleman with a Dog in a Wood* (fig.13) and in later years too, for example in the *Portrait of Gainsborough Dupont* of the 1770s (fig.14).

It is important to remember scale and scaling up in Gainsborough's work of this period. We know that for the most part he worked on a small scale in the 1740s, although, as has been pointed out, he would have had experience of larger formats though working for Hayman on the supper-box paintings for

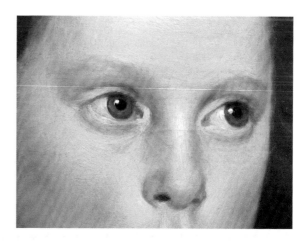

Fig.8
Detail of the girl's face in George Beare's *Portrait of an Elderly Lady and a Girl*, 1747, Yale Center for British Art, Paul Mellon Collection B1976.7.180, New Haven, USA.

Fig.9
Detail of the boy's left hand and cuff in *Portrait of a Boy*, with faint brown brush drawing in the arm and direct tonal application of paint with little blending in the hand,

Fig.10
Detail of brushed brown drawing and unblended tonal application of paint in Thomas Gainsborough, *Mrs Mary Cobbold with her Daughter Anne in a Landscape with a Lamb and Ewe*, Gainsborough's House, Sudbury.

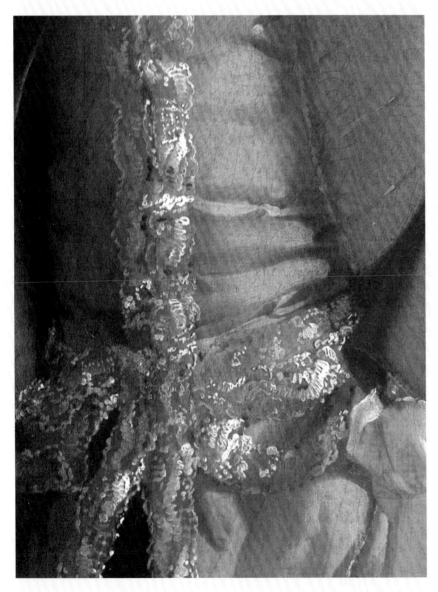

Fig.11
Detail of *Portrait of a Boy:* tonal application of paint in the boy's waistcoat.

Fig.12

Detail of *Portrait of a Boy:* zig-zag brushwork in a self-coloured foreground area.

Fig.12

Detail of *Portrait of a Boy:* zig-zag brushwork in a self-coloured foreground area.

Vauxhall Gardens in 1743.[6] By isolating details, however, one sees familiar patterns, albeit on a different scale, for example this girl's face with the face of Ann Gravenor in *The Gravenor Family* (figs 15–16). Ann Gravenor's face measures only a couple of centimetres in length and was painted with the benefit of perhaps ten years' further experience, but nevertheless one can discern similarities. In the intervening years Gainsborough had learned to articulate the features, making them fit into the facial muscles instead of being stuck onto an oval shape, but the direct gaze and languid eyes remain constant. Graphic impasto describes the lace and the lichen on the tree (fig.17), but on a smaller scale in another painting, where thick impasto was not necessary, we see similar handling (fig.18).

As in all 35 early paintings by Gainsborough examined to date, the colours that were analysed in the paint layers contain ground-up, glassy smalt; in

Fig.13

Detail of *A Gentleman with a Dog in a Wood*, showing zig-zag brushwork in the central, dark green area, which in reality measures c.3 cm across. Private collection on loan to Gainsborough's House.

[6] Belsey, 2002, p.15.

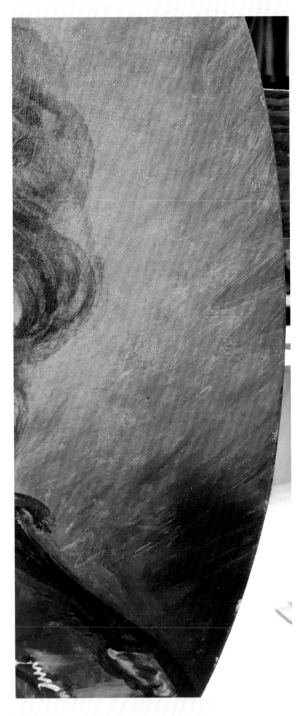

Fig.14
Detail from *Portrait of Gainsborough Dupont*, 1770s, private collection, showing zig-zag brushwork in the background.

this and many other instances smalt was used more as a translucent bulking agent than as a blue colour. Nearly all the colours contain chalk as another bulking agent, again a recurring feature of the early work, along with extensive use of lake pigments – bright, translucent plant dyes that Gainsborough went on to favour throughout his life.[7] The mixtures are complex and some of his pigment particles are very large (fig.19). In addition to the stylistic evidence then, technical analysis makes a very strong case that these fragments were painted by Gainsborough, although alas it cannot bring us closer to the probable date of the painting within the Sudbury period. On the basis of its composition it has been linked with Hogarth's *Mackinen Children* of c.1747 (fig.20).[8] If earlier than Hogarth's painting then, as Hugh Belsey has noted, the painting could draw on common sources, as double portraits of siblings enjoyed popularity in the 1740s.[9] We might bear in mind, however, that we appear to have one instance of Hogarth following the example of young Gainsborough. As discussed in the essay *The Making of Gainsborough's Early Landscapes* (p.89), Hogarth's *O, The Roast Beef of Old England* is unique in his oeuvre in being on an orange coloured ground similar to Gainsborough's *Charterhouse,* which is the earlier of the two paintings.

An interesting feature of this double portrait is that it was painted on a recycled canvas.[10] When the two x-radiographs are placed in the original conformation of the double portrait, an underlying woman's head can be seen straddling the two X-ray images (fig.21). Cross-section samples indicate that her hat, which is similar to that worn by Mrs Andrews in the National Gallery painting (see p.81), was made of straw and that she had grey or powdered hair (fig.22). It is an odd positioning for a single portrait on a canvas this size. If this portrait were perhaps to have been part of a double portrait or a family group, there is no

---

[7] See Rica Jones, *The Making of Gainsborough's Early Landscapes*, this publication, Rica Jones, Gainsborough's Methods and Materials: A 'remarkable ability to make paint sparkle', Young Gainsborough, London, 1997, pp.19–21; Rica Jones, 'The Rev. John Chafy Playing the Violoncello in a Landscape', in Stephen Hackney, Rica Jones and Joyce Townsend (eds), *Paint and Purpose: a Study of Technique in British Art*, Tate Gallery, London, 1999, pp.48–53 and notes pp.203–4; Rica Jones and Martin Postle, 'Gainsborough in his Painting Room, Gainsborough, Tate Gallery Exhibition Catalogue, 2002, pp.30–31.
[8] Elizabeth Einberg, *Hogarth the Painter*, London, Tate Gallery, 1997, pp.46–7.
[9] Belsey, 2002, p.15–16.
[10] First reported in Julian Browne, 'Who's that Girl?', *Sunday Times Colour Supplement*, 16 June 1991, pp.30–32.

Fig.15
Detail of the face in *Portrait of a Girl*.

Fig.16
Detail of Ann Gravenor's face from *The Gravenor Family*,
c.1754 Yale Center for British Art, Paul Mellon Collection
B1977.14.56, New Haven, USA.

Fig.17
Thick impasto detail of lichen on a branch in *Portrait of a Boy*.

Fig.18
Detail of foliage in the background of *A Gentleman with a Dog
in a Wood*. In reality this area is about 5 cm high.

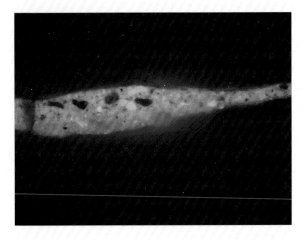

Fig.19
Cross-section sample through green grass in the foreground of *Portrait of a Boy*, photographed at x200 magnification and showing a complex mixture of pigments making up the green colour. Some of the particles (charcoal black and Cologne earth) are very large.

Fig.20
William Hogarth (1697-1764), *Portrait of the Mackinen Children*, c.1747, oil on canvas Photo © National Gallery of Ireland

Fig.21
The two x-radiographs of the fragments in roughly their original position, showing an underlying female head in a straw hat. This image is partially obscured by the boy's cuff and the lichen on a branch at the left edge of his portrait. © Victoria Sutcliffe

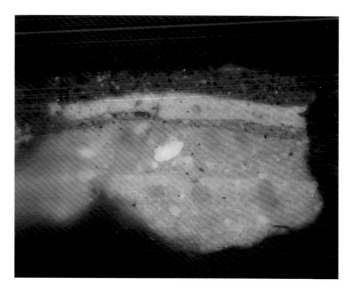

Fig.22

Cross-section sample from the right edge of the girl's portrait, photographed at x200 magnification. Layered structure as shown in the diagram.

Dark green paint of the foliage in the double portrait

Thick straw coloured paint of the womans hat

Opaque, greenish grey paint, perhaps a shadowed area of the underlying womans hair

Second coat of pale grey ground, probably darker than the first

Very thin coat of animal glue size

First coat of pale grey ground

Traces of animal glue size from the canvas

further evidence on the canvas. Apart from her neck, no other part of this sitter or any other appears to have been painted, so we are left in the dark. All the evidence from the X-radiograph and the cross-sections indicates that this woman was painted by Gainsborough.

Finally, can examination of the painting throw any light on its material history and the likely date that the images were separated? As Hugh Belsey has noted, a label on the boy's portrait is dated 1886, by which time we assume the portraits had been separated.[11] Study of the portrait fragments reveals that both have been lined twice.[12] The stretcher and lining of both are in the style of the late nineteenth or early twentieth centuries. Traces of liners' paper tape on the edges of both original canvases are evidence of an earlier lining, probably the lining made necessary when the portraits were cut from their original conformation and then had to be stretched. Postulating a few decades between the two linings, the portraits were probably separated in the early-mid-nineteenth century.

Rica Jones

---

[11] Belsey, 2002, p.15.

[12] Lining involves attaching a new canvas to the back of the original. At this date the adhesive would have been carpenters' glue, applied with heat and pressure.

AN ASSESSMENT OF TWO SMALL PASTORAL LANDSCAPES: *LANDSCAPE WITH DROVER, CATTLE AND DOG* AND *LANDSCAPE WITH SHEPHERD, SHEPHERDESS AND SHEEP*

Rica Jones

These two small landscapes on pine panels (figs 1–2) came to light at auction several years ago, supported by two documents. The first of these is a handwritten paper label attached to the back of the second painting (fig.3). It reads as follows:

> These panels were [bought] at the sale of Mrs Nancy Dickerson of Brook St. Ipswich by Revd. Drury, Claydon, sold by him to Wm. Mason. by him to Mr. J. Soder [or Loder?] whose Mother knew Mrs. Dickerson – Nancy Dickerson was Nancy Good of Sudbury whose Father a Shroud Maker, took Gainsboroughs Father's House and Business
> Tho Spalding Woodbridge
> T.S. [bought] this panel of W. [?]W ————ss Esqr.[1]

The second document, now lost, was a 1970s letter from the then owner saying that in family tradition these two paintings were very early works by Gainsborough and had adorned the door of his father's workroom. John Hayes, quoting part of that letter, illustrated the first panel in the text volume of his catalogue raisonné but did not give the paintings a specific entry in volume two, the catalogue itself.[2] Probably this was because their location far outside Britain meant that he had not seen them. In the caption to the illustration he did, however, date the painting as '*c*.1740(?)', and the presence of their photographs in his files of Suffolk landscapes, rather than those files entitled 'copies and imitations', indicates that he thought favourably of the Gainsborough attribution.[3] In 2017 the opportunity arose to do technical examination of the paintings to judge whether the methods and materials bore any resemblance to Gainsborough's accepted early works.

Both panels measure 230 x 410 mm and their thickness varies from 7 to 10 mm. Both are constructed of two pieces of pine, joined horizontally about 53 mm from the top edge. The wood grain runs horizontally. If the panels once formed one long plank, they were separated before the landscapes were painted, as the

Fig.1
Landscape with Drover, Cattle and Dog, private collection

Fig.2

Landscape with Shepherd, Shepherdess and Sheep, private collection.

images do not join up seamlessly; a gap of about 10 cm is needed for the lines of the two landscapes to match up. Except where worn by abrasion here and there, the paint covers the whole of each panel, forming a soft meniscus at the extreme edge, indicating that the panels were not held in a rebated system when the landscapes were painted. In Figure 4 we see the lower edge of one of the panels viewed at high magnification. It is clear that both paintings are on recycled timber; three phases of painting are visible underneath the image that we see in normal viewing. The first, applied directly to the panel, is a plain coat of lean white paint; this is what we would now call an undercoat or priming. On top of that is a semi-translucent coat of reddish brown paint; study of cross-section samples (fig.5) shows that the underlying white paint was dry when the reddish brown was applied and that this layer is of uneven thickness. The reddish brown colour is covered over with a thick coat of opaque powder blue paint, which has shrunk into an 'alligator skin' pattern of cracks all over both

panels, leaving the reddish brown paint visible at the base of each crack. The reason behind this development is that the reddish brown colour is actually a lacquer, which is to say oil paint mixed with a resin to render it translucent.[4] Pure oil paint such as the powder blue cannot properly grip an underlying resinous paint and eventually develops a network of shrinkage cracks such as those we see in this instance. The pastoral image was done on top of the powder blue and has itself been pulled apart by the underlying system of cracks.

Were the underlying coats of paint self-coloured or modulated as designs in some way? Close examination of the paint surface and of cross-section samples indicates that they were self-coloured, but the reddish brown lacquer was modulated by combing to mimic wood graining. Overall the evidence strongly suggests that these pieces of wood were once part of a panelled interior, which was repainted from time to time, as we redecorate rooms today.

---

[1] To date, it has not been possible to find specific documentation for Nancy Good or her husband Mr Dickerson, although both surnames occur in and around Sudbury. There were three generations who were Revd. Drury of Claydon, spanning 100 years. I am grateful to Fiona Atkins for this last information.

[2] John Hayes, *The Landscape Paintings of Thomas Gainsborough,* London, 1982, vol.1, p.31.

[3] Paul Mellon Centre for Studies in British Art, London, John Hayes Archive, JTH /5/14 parts 1 and 2.

[4] When the cross-sections are viewed in ultraviolet light, the reddish brown layer fluoresces opaque white, suggesting a resinous content, perhaps even a hard resin such as copal or sandarac rather than a soft resin such as mastic.

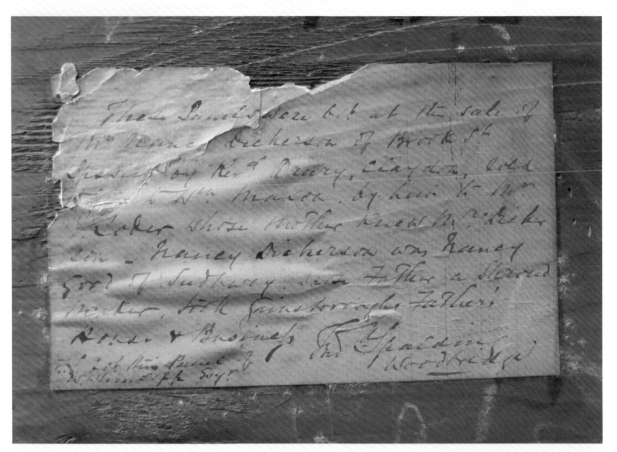

Fig.3
Label on the back of
*Landscape with Shepherd,
Shepherdess and Sheep.*

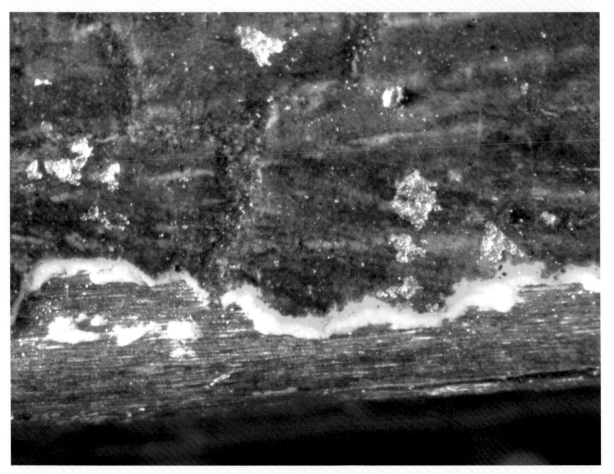

Fig.4
*Landscape with Shepherd,
Shepherdess and Sheep,*
photographed at x10
magnification. Where the
paint is worn on the lower
edge of the pine panel we
can see the white undercoat,
reddish brown lacquer at the
base of the cracks, powder
blue paint, and the final
image, with traces of gilding
from a later frame.

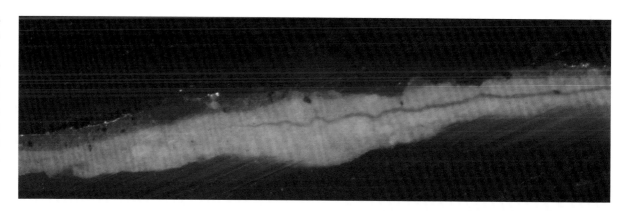

Fig.5
Cross-section sample from the same area as fig.4, photographed at x200 magnification and showing all the layers. The reddish brown lacquer is the translucent layer of uneven thickness above the white undercoat.

Is it possible that these paintings, given their documented provenance from the house in which Gainsborough spent his boyhood, are by the very young Thomas Gainsborough, perhaps in his early teens on vacation home from his training in London? While we do not have much by way of strict comparison, their content and handling bear some similarity to known technical features of his work. Firstly the use of wooden panel, while unusual throughout British painting at this period, is not unknown, and there is one accepted example from Gainsborough's *oeuvre*, dated roughly 1748–50.[5] The small *Self Portrait with Palette,* a very early work, is painted on card that had been used for painting twice before.[6] So the re-use of a couple of bits of old panelling would be in keeping with accepted examples of Gainsborough's juvenile work.

The second feature that chimes with Gainsborough's technical practice is the presence of certain pigments that are unusual for the period among British painters: lead-tin yellow is present in several samples, ditto the mineral-based blue azurite, and white dolomite, which is limestone. The greens and yellows contain significant amounts of lake pigments, which is to say translucent pigments based on plant dyes. The blue glassy pigment, smalt, is present in many samples, not just as a colour but as a transparent extender; chalk is also present for the same function; both are regular features of Gainsborough's early work.[7] The mixtures

Fig.6
Dark bluish green paint from *Landscape with Drover, Cattle and Dog,* photographed at x25 magnification, showing complex mixtures of pigments and large particles.

of pigments that produce one colour are complex, as they would be all his life, and they incorporate large particles, as seen in Figure 6, photographed through the microscope, and at larger magnification in Figure 13 in *The Making of Gainsborough's Early Landscapes* (p.95).

Stylistically, for all their charmingly naïve character, these paintings display features that become characteristic of his work. Firstly there is the graphic depiction of light and shade in unblended colours, as seen in Figure 7. The highlights and shadows in the drover and his animals all have distinct colours, which

[5] Hayes, 1982, vol.2, pp.355 and 377.

[6] Unpublished technical report by Rica Jones, 2001. For illustration see M. Rosenthal and M. Myrone (eds), *Gainsborough,* exhibition catalogue, Tate Britain, London 2002, p.45.

[7] See Rica Jones, *The Making of Gainsborough's Early Landscapes,* Rica Jones, 'Gainsborough's Methods and Materials: A 'remarkable ability to make paint sparkle', in *Young Gainsborough,* London, 1997, pp.19–21; Rica Jones, 'The Rev. John Chafy Playing the Violoncello in a Landscape', in Stephen Hackney, Rica Jones and Joyce Townsend (eds), *Paint and Purpose: a Study of Technique in British Art,* Tate Gallery, London, 1999, pp.48–53 and notes pp.203–4; Rica Jones and Martin Postle, 'Gainsborough in his Painting Room, *Gainsborough,* exhibition catalogue, Tate, London, 2002, pp.30–31.

Fig.7
Detail from *Landscape with Drover, Cattle and Dog*, showing highlights and shadows laid on in graphic fashion and hardly blended. The underlying network of cracks has affected all but the thickest paint

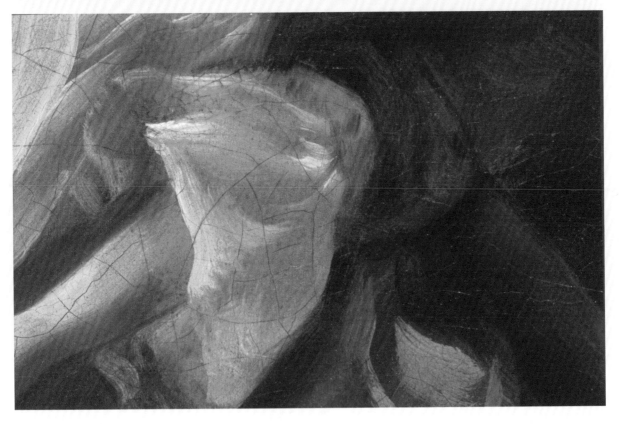

Fig.8
Close-up detail from Mrs Gravenor's sleeve and skirt, from Thomas Gainsborough, *The Gravenor Family*, c.1752, Yale Center for British Art, New Haven, USA. In reality this area is about 12 cm square.

are laid on in a graphic description of their respective shapes and hardly blended together. This is how Gainsborough perceived and represented volume in the first decade or so of his work, for example in Figure 8, a close-up of brushwork from *The Gravenor Family*. Another characteristic feature is the textured depiction of tree trunks and foliage, as seen in Figure 9 and in Figure 4 in *The Making of Gainsborough's Early Landscapes*. Again these features occur in his work all his life, together with very direct, competent use of the brush. All in all then, there is a good deal of stylistic and technical evidence to support the documentation that these two landscapes were painted by a very young Thomas Gainsborough.

Rica Jones

Fig.9
Detail of tree trunks and foliage in *Landscape with Shepherd, Shepherdess and Sheep*, photographed in raking light from the left

PP. 5459. 3

THE EUROPEAN MAGAZINE,

AND London Review:

Containing the

Literature, HISTORY, Politics,

Arts, Manners & Amusements of the Age;

Simul et jucunda et idonea dicerevitæ.

BY THE

Philological Society of London.

VOL. XIV. for 1788.

Shepherd

sculpsit.

LONDON:

Printed for J. Sewell, Cornhill 1788.

APPENDIX I:
THE OBITUARIES IN *THE EUROPEAN MAGAZINE*

The first known written account of Gainsborough's early life appeared in the *Morning Herald* just two days after his death on Monday 4 August. It is generally accepted that this was written by Sir Henry Bate Dudley, the paper's editor and a close friend of Gainsborough. 'It is safe to say,' Whitley wrote, 'that no painter has ever been so consistently supported by a daily newspaper as Gainsborough was by the *Morning Herald* from 1781 to 1788'.[1] The obituary, like Bate Dudley's other commentaries of Gainsborough's work, is sympathetic and laudatory. It gives a balanced picture in thirteen paragraphs, beginning and ending with declarations, the opening describing him as 'one of the greatest geniuses that ever adorned any age' and ending with praising his virtues as a man. In between, his death is described in detail, and before his formative years, time in London, Bath and return to the metropolis, is followed by a reflection on his portraiture, landscapes and fancy pictures interwoven with his royal patronage. It gives a picture of a young artist from humble but virtuous origins achieving the heights of fame through his genius. The obituary set the mark for the numerous ones that followed.

On the following day 5 August, *The Morning Chronicle* and *The Times* both published Bate-Dudley's obituary in its entirety, with only a few abbreviations, such as the paragraph dealing with the manner of his death.[2] It was also repeated during the next few days in a number of papers throughout the country including the *Kentish Gazette*, *Chelmsford Chronicle* and *London Chronicle*, with shorter versions in the *Northampton Mercury*, *Oxford Journal* and others.[3] *The Morning Post* published a note on Gainsborough on 5 August and although it did not repeat in full Bate Dudley's obituary it followed its spirit, praising the artist's ability in landscape and portraiture, which combined 'an excellence in two different provinces of his art which the same individual has seldom attained ...'. It also praised the man, for 'whatever his abilities as a painter, he was eminently distinguished for private virtues, and in the domestic and convivial sphere, without deviating into weakness on the one hand, or excess on the other, possessed'.[4]

If Bate Dudley's eulogistic words dominated the majority of the week after Gainsborough's death, the Friday edition of the *Morning Chronicle* chose to follow on from its reprint of this biography, with its own lengthy account.[5] It is not known who authored this account, which is further confused as it is so often mixed up with Bate Dudley's earlier words in a large number of later articles and books that mix the two obituaries. The editor of the paper in 1788 was William Woodfall (bap.1745–1803) and the writer of the article was clearly a friend of Gainsborough, not only because of his clear familiarity with the artist, but also by his stating within the text that 'He [Gainsborough] told the writer of this article ...'. The opening of the obituary makes clear its intent: 'Of Mr. Gainsborough's birth and lamented death you have already told us; with the circumstances that introduced him to the world as a Painter, the public are not generally acquainted'. The content is particularly important for any consideration of Gainsborough's early life because of the level of details it offers of this period and its deep understanding of Gainsborough's practice. It clearly must have been someone close to him. Following Bate Dudley's outline sketch, it offers insights into how he learnt to become a painter, the practical issues he faced as an artist and a thoughtful reflection on his portraits and his depictions of the natural world. It has also arguably been far more influential on the way we think about Gainsborough's development as an artist, and also introduces to the public for the first time, the anecdote about the Tom Peartree.

[1] William Whitley, 'An Eighteenth-century Art Chronicler: Sir Henry Bate Dudley, Bart.', *The Walpole Society*, 1925, vol. XIII, Oxford, p.40.

[2] *Morning Chronicle*, issue 6003, 5 August 1788, p.4; *The Times*, 5 August 1788, p.4.

[3] *London Chronicle*, 7 August 1788, p.126; *Bury and Norwich Post*, 6 August 1788, p.2; *Kentish Gazette*, Friday 8 August 1788, p.2; *Ipswich Journal*, 9 August 1788; *Chelmsford Chronicle*, 8 August 1788, p.2; *Northampton Mercury*, 9 August 1788, p.1; *Oxford Journal*, 9 August 1788, p.1.

[4] 'Obituary, Thomas Gainsborough', *The Morning Post*, 5 August 1788, p.2.

[5] *Morning Chronicle*, 'Mr Gainsborough, the Painter', issue 6006, 8 August 1788, p.3.

Only one of the three biographies bears an author's name: Philip Thicknesse in his *A Sketch of the Life of and Paintings of Thomas Gainsborough, Esq.* Not bound by the modesty that he saw in Gainsborough, Thicknesse presented himself as the great discoverer of genius, as he expressed it: 'I can with truth boast, that I was the first man who perceived; though through clouds of bad colouring, what an accurate eye he possessed ... and who dragged him from the obscurity of a Country Town...' to be 'acknowledged by all lovers of the Arts, and envied even by the FIRST ARTISTS his Contemporaries ...'.[6] The book was hastily published through the printseller Samuel Fores, who had published other works by Thicknesse and had a long-standing relationship with him.[7] An essential skill for a printseller was the ability to turn things around quickly and there is little doubt that Thicknesse wished to publish as soon as possible to make his name synonymous with the artist.

The exact date of its release is difficult to gauge, particularly as it appears to be in two distinct sections, the first ending with 'lamented by all who knew him, and has left a fame behind him which can NEVER DIE'.[8] The new section starts (it is the only full line spacing in the book) with 'Since most of these pages were printed off, I have seen a long and very excellent account of Mr. Gainsborough and his paintings, in the gentleman's magazine for August last'.[9] It implies that Thicknesse's book appeared in two editions, the first influencing obituaries and the second, which included corrections and additions as a result of later obituaries. The *Gentleman's Magazine* must have seen the first part (or first edition) of Thicknesse's text to include so many references to Thicknesse and specific details of Gainsborough's life previously unpublished.[10] In the second part (or second edition) he took issue with the early account of Gainsborough's life and takes it upon himself to correct them, 'there are however some

trifling mistakes which I think ought to be rectified, as well as an omission of my own'.[11] The details of the early life were already being contested.

It is worth noting here that the lengthy and full obituaries in the *Gentleman's Magazine* and the *European Magazine,* published in their August editions, were amalgamations of all three accounts. The *European Magazine,* publishing the first two obituaries one after another almost unchanged with some notes from Thicknesse concluding the article. The *Gentleman's Magazine* uses the same material but mixes it together to make a largely chronological account and probably because of that has largely been taken as the definitive obituary, by those unaware that it is an amalgamation of three separate texts.

Thicknesse was keen to position Gainsborough's death as the passing of a great genius, just as the other obituaries were. His motives however seem largely driven by self-interest and monopolising on the opportunity of the artist's demise, through positioning himself as the great artistic impresario who had discovered Gainsborough, guiding him to become the genius he became. Thicknesse also added to his credentials, with the following offer: 'he gave me this, his that he gave me this, his MAIDEN DRAWING... it shall be left with the publisher of this book ten days, for the inspection of the curious, and the confirmation of the truth of what I have advanced.'[12]

In establishing the sources of the earliest accounts of the young Gainsborough; their publication and authorship where possible, we are able to read and interpret them in a much clearer way. From Bate Dudley, through an unknown friend, to Thicknesse and his revisions, we can use this information to give a convincing account of Gainsborough's early life.

Mark Bills

---

[6] Philip Thicknesse, *A Sketch of the Life of and Paintings of Thomas Gainsborough, Esq.*, London, 1788, pp.3–4.

[7] See Mark Bills, *Samuel William Fores: Satirist*, Sudbury, Gainsborough's House, 2014.

[8] Thicknesse, 1788, p.51.

[9] Thicknesse, 1788, p.51.

[10] A good example of this is: 'When Mr. Thicknesse was first appointed lieutenant governor of Languard Fort, he found Mr. G. dwelling in a house of six pounds a year rent at Ipswich' in the *Gentleman's Magazine*, August 1788, p.753, and '... he retired to Ipswich in Suffolk, took a small house of six pounds a year in that Town ... Soon after his remove to Ipswich I was appointed Lieutenant Governor of Land Guard Fort', in Thicknesse, 1788, p.9.

[11] Thicknesse, 1788, p.51.

[12] Thicknesse, 1788, pp.6–7. If there was a separate first edition it would mean that the drawing was at Fores' shop in Piccadilly for the middle and end of August 1788.

Contents Page, *The European Magazine and London Review*, VOL. XIV for 1788, Printed by J.Sewell, Cornhill
© British Library Board P.P.5459.z

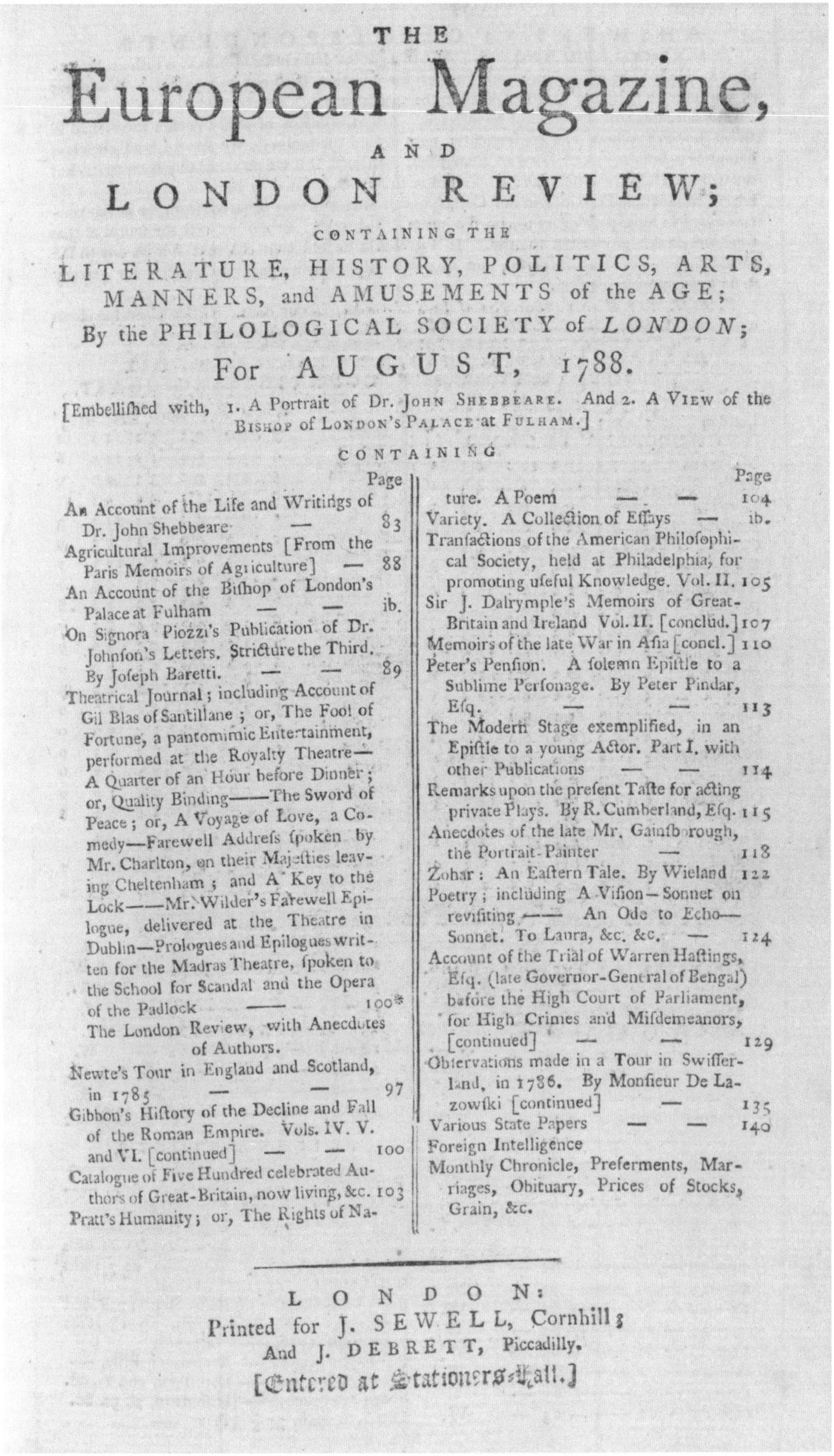

THE
European Magazine,
AND
LONDON REVIEW;

CONTAINING THE

LITERATURE, HISTORY, POLITICS, ARTS, MANNERS, and AMUSEMENTS of the AGE;

By the PHILOLOGICAL SOCIETY of *LONDON*;

For AUGUST, 1788.

[Embellished with, 1. A Portrait of Dr. JOHN SHEBBEARE. And 2. A VIEW of the BISHOP OF LONDON'S PALACE at FULHAM.]

CONTAINING

LONDON:
Printed for J. SEWELL, Cornhill;
And J. DEBRETT, Piccadilly.
[Entered at Stationers-Hall.]

Page 118, *The European Magazine and London Review*, VOL. XIV for 1788, Printed by J.Sewell, Cornhill
© British Library Board P.P.5459.z

country house or palace: neither should the spectators be totally excused from their subscription to the general *gala*, nor left to dose upon their benches through the progress of five tedious acts, but called upon at intervals by music, dance or refreshment, elegantly contrived, to change the sameness of the scene, and relieve the efforts of the more active corps employed upon the drama.

And now let me say one word to qualify the irony I set out with, and acquit myself as a moralist.

There are many and great authorities against this species of entertainment, and certainly the danger is great, where theatrical propensities are too much indulged in young and inexperienced minds. Tertullian says, (but he is speaking of a very licentious theatre) *Theatrum sacrarium est Veneris*—" A playhouse is the very sacristy of Venus." And Juvenal, who wrote in times of the grossest impurity, maintains that no prudent man will take any young lady to wife, who has ever been even within the walls of a theatre.—

Cuneis an habent spectacula totis
Quod securas ames, quodque inde excerpere possis?

" Look round, and say if any man of sense
" Will dare to single out a wife from hence?

Young women of humble rank and small pretensions should be particularly cautious how a vain ambition of being noticed by their superiors betrays them into an attempt at displaying their unprotected persons on a stage, however dignified and respectable. If they have talents, and of course applause, are their understandings and manners proof against applause? If they mistake their talents, and merit no applause, are they sure they will get no contempt for their self-conceit? If they have both acting talents and attractive charms, I tremble for their danger. Let the foolish parent, whose itching ears tingled with the plaudits that resounded through the theatre, where virgin modesty deposited its blushes, beware how his aching heart shall throb with sorrow, when the daughter, *quæ pudica ad theatrum accesserat, inde revertetur impudica. (Cyprian. ad Donatum.)*

So much by way of caution to the guardians and protectors of innocence; let the offence light where it may, I care not, so it serves the cause for which my heart is pledged.

As for my opinion of private plays in general, though it is a fashion which hath kings and princes for its nursing fathers, and queens and princesses for its nursing mothers, I think it is a fashion that should be cautiously indulged, and narrowly confined to certain ranks, ages and conditions in the community at large. Grace forbid! that what the author of my motto said scoffingly of the Greeks should be said prophetically of this nation. Emulate them in their love of freedom, in their love of science; rival them in the greatest of their actions, but not in the versatility of their mimic talents, till it shall be said of us by some future satirist,—

Natio comœda est. Rides? Majore cachinno
Concutitur: flet, si lacrymas aspexit amici,
Nec dolet. Igniculum brumæ si tempore poscas,
Accipit endromidem: Si dixeris, æstuo, sudat.
Nos sumus ergo pares; melior qui semper et omni
Nocte dieque potest alienum sumere vultum.

" Laugh, and your merry echo bursts his
        sides;
" Weep, and his courteous tears gush out in
        tides:
" Light a few sticks you cry, 'tis wintry-Lo!
" He's a furr'd Laplander from top to toe;
" Put out the fire, for now 'tis warm—
        He's more,
" Hot, sultry hot, and sweats at every pore:
" Oh! he's beyond us; we can make no
        race
" With one, who night and day maintains
        his pace,
" And fast as you shift humours still can
        shift his face."

ANECDOTES of the late Mr. GAINSBOROUGH, the PORTRAIT-PAINTER.

SATURDAY morning, August 2, about two o'clock, died, at his house in Pall-mall, Mr. GAINSBOROUGH, the Painter, one of the greatest geniuses that ever adorned any age, or any nation!

His dissolution was occasioned by a cancer in the neck; the effects of which became violent a few months since, owing to a cold caught one morning in Westminster Hall, while attending the trial of Mr. Hastings.

Mr. Gainsborough a very few weeks since was in the vigour of his professional powers. He was just turned of 61 years of age. He was born at Sudbury, in Suffolk, in the year 1727.—His father, on his outset in life, was possessed of a decent competency; but a large family, and liberal heart, soon lessened his wealth to a very humble income.

The son of whom we speak, very early discovered a propensity to painting. Nature
                                                            was

Page 119, *The European Magazine and London Review*, VOL. XIV for 1788, Printed by J.Sewell, Cornhill
© British Library Board P.P.5459.z

was his teacher, and the Woods of Suffolk his Academy. Here he would pass in solitude his mornings, in making a sketch of an antiquated tree, a marshy brook, a few cattle, a shepherd and his flock, or any other accidental objects that were presented.

From delineation he got to colouring; and after painting several landscapes from the age of ten to twelve, he quitted Sudbury in his 13th year, and came to London, where he commenced portrait-painter; and from that time never cost his family the least expence. The person at whose house he principally resided, was a silversmith of some taste, and from him he was ever ready to confess he derived great assistance. Mr. Gravelot the engraver was also his patron, and got him introduced at the Old Academy of the Arts, in St. Martin's-lane. He continued to exercise his pencil in London for some years, but marrying Mrs. Gainsborough when he was only nineteen years of age, he soon after took up his residence at Ipswich; and after practising there for a considerable period, went to Bath, where his friends intimated his merits would meet their proper reward.

His portrait of Quin, the actor, which he painted at Bath about thirty years since, will be ever considered as a wonderful effort in the portrait line; and it is with a degree of veneration that Mr. Gainsborough always spoke of Mr. Ralph Allen, Earl Camden, and a few other gentlemen, for the patronage and favour they extended to him here.

The high reputation which followed, prompted him to return to London, where he arrived in the year 1774.—After passing a short time in town not very profitably, his merit engaged the attention of the King. Among other portraits of the Royal Family, the full length of his Majesty at the Queen's House, will ever be viewed as an astonishing performance. From this period, Mr. Gainsborough entered in a line which afforded a becoming reward to his superlative powers.

All our living Princes and Princesses have been painted by him, the Duke of York excepted, of whom he had three pictures bespoken; and among his latter performances the head of Mr. Pitt and several portraits of that gentleman's family afforded him gratification.

His portraits will pass to futurity with a reputation equal to that which follows the pictures of Vandyke; and his landscapes will establish his name on the record of the fine arts, with honours such as never before attended a native of this isle.

The landscape of the Woodman in the Storm, finished about eighteen months since, and now at his rooms in Pall-mall, for expression, character, and beautiful colouring, is of inestimable worth.——His Majesty's praises of this Picture made Mr. Gainsborough feel trebly elate:—and the attention of the Queen, who sent to him soon after, and commissioned him to paint the Duke of York, were circumstances that he always dwelt upon with conscious pleasure.

The few pictures he attempted that are stiled Sea Pieces, may be recurred to, in proof of his power in painting water: nothing can exceed them in transparency and air.

But he is gone!—and while we lament him as an artist, let us not pass over those virtues, which were an honour to human nature!—Let a tear be shed in affection for that generous heart,—whose strongest propensities were to relieve the claims of poverty, wherever they appeared genuine!—His liberality was not confined to this alone,—needy relatives and unfortunate friends were further incumbrances on a spirit, that could not deny.

It only remains to say, that an universality of powers adorned his mind.

His Epistolary Correspondence possessed the ease of Swift, and the nervous force of Bolingbroke;—and a selection of his letters would offer to the world as much originality and beauty, as is even to be traced in his Painting!

In conversation, his ideas and expression discovered a mind full of rich fancies and elegant truths—and it is not an aggravation to say, that two of the first writers of this age, Mr. Sheridan and Mr. Tickell, have frequently been witnesses of the most astonishing bursts of genius from him at these moments; and never fail to bear testimony of his pregnant imagination.

The science to which he was principally attached, besides Painting, was Music:—He was skilled in all keyed instruments,—but was most strongly attached to stringed ones. His performance on the Viola da Gamba was in some movements equal to the touch of Abel. He always play'd to the feelings; but as he hated parade, he never could be prevailed upon to display this talent, except to his most select friends.

***

" *By Heaven, and not a Master taught.*"

OF Mr. GAINSBOROUGH's birth and lamented death you have already told us; with the circumstances that introduced him to the world as a Painter, the public are not generally acquainted.

In the neighbourhood of his father was a very respectable Clergyman, of the name of Coyte. With the sons of this gentleman young Gainsborough and his brothers passed much of their time, and from the instructions of the old man reaped some advantage. In

one

Page 120, *The European Magazine and London Review*, VOL. XIV for 1788, Printed by J.Sewell, Cornhill
© British Library Board P.P.5459.z

one of these visits there happened a violent commotion in the family, on account of the Parson's garden having been plundered of a great quantity of wall fruit, and much pains was taken, but without effect, to discover the thief. Young Gainsborough having one summer morning risen at an early hour, and walked into the garden to make a sketch from an old elm, seated himself in an obscure corner, and had just taken out his chalk to begin, when he observed a fellow's head peeping over the wall of the garden, which was next the road, with an apparent intention of seeing if the coast was clear. This changed the young Tyro's object, and instead of sketching the elm, he, in the few moments before he was himself observed, made a sketch upon a rough board of the head of the man; and so accurate was the resemblance, that he was instantly known to be a man from a neighbouring village, and upon a close enquiry proved to be the fellow who had before robbed the garden. This was shewn about the village, and considered as a strong proof of a genius above the common standard: the young Coytes lent him their drawing-books, and the boy shewing extreme eagerness in the pursuit, wandering through fields, meadows, and woods, in search of rural scenes, became talked of in the neighbourhood; and there not being any body in the country who could properly instruct him in his studies, he was very soon afterwards sent to London, and here made his first essays in art, by modelling figures of cows, horses, and dogs, in which he attained very great excellence: there is a cast in the plaister shops from an old horse that he modelled, which has peculiar merit. He soon after became a pupil to Mr. Gravelot, under whose instructions he drew most of the ornaments which decorate the illustrious heads so admirably engraved by Houbraken, which were they as faithful in their resemblance as they are exquisite in their execution, would be curious and useful to the phisiognomist, as well as they are to the collector; but unfortunately these heads were copied by boys, and very frequently from unascertained portraits, sent to Holland to be engraved by Houbraken, and when returned, dignified with any illustrious name which Mr. Knapton, the publisher, thought proper. Thurlow's and about thirty of the others are copied from heads painted for no one knew who. But to return to Mr. Gainsborough: his first efforts were small landscapes, which he frequently sold to the dealers at trifling prices; and when he afterwards engaged in portraits, his price was from three to five guineas; but as he extended his fame he advanced his prices: and it may be added, that

his powers advanced in nearly equal proportion, for his early portraits have very little to recommend them. Since his return from Bath, as well as before, the portraits of his gentlemen have been very superior to those of his ladies, which being frequently designed from women that were painted, gave a general appearance to all his females of painted women.

His portraits of the Angels of the Court frequently gave us as much the idea of Angels as they could do, from having no particle of a gross, earthy, or substantial form about them. But in his portraits of men imitation assumes the energy of life. He seems almost the only painter of this country, who attempts the thin brilliant stile of pencilling of Vandyke; and yet with all this blaze of excellence, with all this accuracy of resemblance, (and he gives not merely the map of the face, but the character, the soul of the original) his likenesses are attained by the indecision more than the precision of the outlines. He gives the feature and the shadow, so that it is sometimes not easy to say which is which; for the scumbling about the feature sometimes looks like the feature itself; so that he shews the face in more points of view than one, and by that means it strikes every one who has once seen the original with being a resemblance: so that while the portrait with a rigid outline exhibits the countenance only in one disposition of mind, he gives it in many. His portraits are calculated to give effect at a distance; and that effect is produced in so eminent a degree, that the picture may almost be mistaken for the original: but closely inspected, we wonder at the delusion, and find scumbling scratches that have no appearance of eye-brows or nostrils. He told the writer of this article, that he never found any portrait so difficult to hit as that of the late Mr. Garrick; for when he was sketching in the eye-brows, and thought he had hit upon the precise situation, and looked a second time at his model, he found the eye-brows lifted up to the middle of his forehead; and when he a third time looked, they were dropped like a curtain close over the eye: so flexible and universal was the countenance of this great player, that it was as impossible to catch his likeness as it is to catch the form of a passing cloud. This portrait did not do any honour to either artist or comedian. Very different is the full-length portrait of Mr. Abel, with the dog under the table, which combines with the force of a sketch the high finishing of a miniature. To this may be added many others of equal merit, though not finished with equal delicacy. Indeed, finishing was not his aim: we may almost say it was not in general possible to him, for he

usually

Page 121, *The European Magazine and London Review*, VOL. XIV for 1788, Printed by J.Sewell, Cornhill
© British Library Board P.P.5459.z

usually painted with a very long and very broad brush, stood very far from his canvas, and in a room with very little light. Portraits were not his forte, his fame rests on better ground, upon an almost unparalleled extent of talent in landscapes, animals, and figures. By figures I do not mean the well drest high powdered gentlemen of St. James's, but the rustic, the peasant, the shepherd's boy, and cottage girl. Here nature appears as in a mirror, and in these little simple subjects a story is told that awakens the most pathetic sensations, and equally evinces the truth, taste, and genius of the master. In his landscapes he has at different times assumed the manner of many different artists, and during the time he adhered to them equalled them all, and in some of his latter pictures so far united these different stiles as to form one grand whole, peculiarly his own, and peculiarly excellent.

The first master he studied was Wynants, whose thistles and dock leaves he has frequently introduced into his early pictures. The next was Ruysdale, but his colouring is less sombre, though the pencilling of the Englishman was less accurate than that of the Fleming. He has sometimes very happily seized upon the best manner of Teniers, and may like that artist be very properly called the Proteus of painting. In a view of company in St. James's Park he assumed the manner of Watteau, and produced a picture in many respects superior to any Watteau ever painted. Of the animals of Snyders he thought with admiration, and seems to have made that master his model, though excellently as he painted animals he never equalled that great artist. From a picture of Morillio he copied the figure of an infant Christ, which was engraved by Major, and is in effect not inferior to the original. In one of his landscapes he has taken the idea of a Country Church-Yard from Mr. Gray, and the solemnity of the scene and situation of the figures have a most picturesque and poetical effect; but Mr. Gainsborough was not a man of reading, nor was the figure of Lavinia, which was lately exhibited, painted from Thomson's character (for at the time the figure was painted, it is probable he had never read the book) but a little simple character from his own imagination. The figures, animals, and trees of his latter landscapes are not finished in the manner they were formerly. They have a more powerful effect, with less labour, and evince more genius with less pains. He was not the painter for the botanist; he did not minutely describe every fibre of a dock leaf, but gave those general resemblances which strike every eye. A bank spread with weeds and wild flowers; a stump of an old tree, which a gentleman would grub out of his estate; a cottage with scarce thatch enough to keep out the rain, were objects which he delighted in, and from which he produced interesting and delightful effects, though when closely inspected they appear mere blots.

His musical taste was perhaps equal to that of any one of his cotemporaries, and he himself thought he was not intended by nature for a painter, but for a musician. His fondness for the art was most enthusiastic, and he would frequently seclude himself from all society, for weeks together, for the sole purpose of practising it.

Mr. GAINSBOROUGH, a very few weeks before his death, and at a time when he considered his duration in life of *less* permanency than he even did the day before he expired[*],—wrote some observations relative to his funeral, that his family might be as little perplexed as possible on so distressing a subject.

" He desired he might be privately buried " in Kew Church-yard, near the grave of his " friend Mr. KIRBY;—that a stone, with- " out either arms or ornament, might be " placed over him;—inscribed with his bare " name, and containing space for the names " of such of his family who, after death, " might wish to take up their abode with " him;——and that his funeral might be " as private as possible, and attended only " by a few of those friends he most respect- " ed."

In obedience to these injunctions, on the 9th inst. Mr. GAINSBOROUGH's Remains were conveyed from his house in Pall-mall to Kew.—He was attended by the following gentlemen:

Mr. Sheridan,	Mr. Paul Sandby,
Sir Joshua Reynolds,	Mr. Cotes,
Sir Wm. Chambers,	Mr. Myers,
Mr. John Hunter,	Mr. Gossett,
Mr. Linley,	Mr. Buttall,
Mr. West,	Mr. Pearce,
Mr. Bartolozzi,	Mr. Trimmer.
Mr. Dupont,	

The pall in the procession to the church was sustained by Sir Joshua Reynolds, Sir

---

[*] Mr. Gainsborough's disorder was a wen, and not a cancer, as before erroneously stated, which grew internally, and so large as to obstruct the passages. This, it is said, his surgeons knew, but knew at the same time it was fatal to attempt to cut it. It has, however, been extracted since his decease, and put in again.

Page 122, *The European Magazine and London Review*, VOL. XIV for 1788, Printed by J. Sewell, Cornhill

© British Library Board P.P.5459.z

William Chambers, Mr. West, Mr. Bartolozzi, Mr. Cotes, and Mr. P. Sandby. Mr. Dupont, the nephew and pupil of Mr. Gainsborough †, attended as chief mourner.

ZOHAR: An EASTERN TALE,
By WIELAND.

IN the infancy of the world mankind knew no other restraints than those imposed by nature. No throne was erected on the ruins of liberty; and men had not learnt, like the beasts, to bend their necks to the yoke of men. Each took up his abode on the spot that most pleased him, without fear of being disturbed, and the earth bestowed on him her fruits with liberality, which he did not abuse. In those happy times lived Zohar, on whom fortune was prodigal of her gifts. She had placed him not far from the banks of the Euphrates, in a country adorned with unceasing verdure, where a thousand rivulets winded through flowery vallies and meadows covered with flocks. He possessed whole forests of palm-trees; he enjoyed a numerous houshold, and all the treasures of simplicity. It is easy to conceive how great might have been his felicity; for no man on earth will be unsatisfied with his lot, provided he listens to the voice of his Internal Instructor. To be happy, the wise have no occasion for the abundance of Zohar. Though this young man had received from nature a benevolent heart and a chearful mind, yet the fervour of unrestrained youth soon made him quit the path of rectitude, led him into innumerable errors, and inspired him with innumerable desires. He found nothing but tedious uniformity in the happy state he enjoyed. New wishes and new desires succeeded to those he had just formed, and these in their turn gave place to others in perpetual succession. What was to be done in such a case? Notwithstanding the riches of nature, she is always too poor to satisfy the desires of the unreasonable. But disgust itself, by leading them to reflection, often frees them from the misery of ceaseless craving. One day as Zohar, tired with vain wishes, had sunk to sleep, a lively dream continued the train of his ideas. Firnaz, the spirit to whom the King of the Genii has subjected our globe, undertook to cure this young man of his delusion.

Zohar thought himself placed on the summit of a mountain, from whence, reclined at the foot of a cedar, he surveyed the possessions of his ancestors extended far and wide. But, instead of viewing them with pleasure, he broke forth at the sight into bitter complaints. The meads were enamelled with flowers, the rivulets murmured through the palm-trees, the hills were white with sheep, and shone like the marble of Paros; but they shone not for Zohar.

Assaulted by a thousand different desires, he was wandering with uncertain steps, when his eyes were suddenly dazzled by a light of unusual splendor. A cloud of gold and azure descended from the sky diffusing around the most grateful fragrance. On this cloud was seated a celestial figure, whose look and gracious smile prevented the disquiet which

---

† Mr. Gainsborough had a brother, who was a dissenting minister at Henley upon Thames, that possessed as strong a genius for mechanics, as the artist had for painting. When he died, which was about four or five years ago, all his models of machines, dials, engines, &c. came into the hands of Mr. Gainsborough, of Pall-mall, who gave them to Mr. Thicknesse. Among them was a clock of a very peculiar construction; it told the hour by a little ball, and was kept in motion by a leaden bullet, which dropped from a spiral reservoir at the top of the clock into a little ivory bucket. This was so contrived as to discharge it at the bottom, and by means of a counter weight was carried up to the top of the clock, where it received another bullet, which was discharged as the former. This was evidently an attempt at the perpetual motion, which he thought attainable. There was also the model of a steam engine, which a crafty man surreptitiously obtained a sight of and pirated; and a curious sun-dial, the apparatus of which could not have been made by a mathematical instrument-maker for fifty guineas. The sun-dial Mr. Thicknesse presented to the British Museum, and he had the Governors thanks for enriching it with so valuable a curiosity. It is very well worthy of the inspection of the curious. Mr. T. was willing enough to part with it, yet wished to place it where it might remain as long as brass or iron can endure. The clock Mr. Thicknesse has, with other works, at his own house at Bath. Few men were ever more respected than this worthy Divine; he was as eminent for humanity, simplicity, and integrity, as he was for genius. Mr. Gainsborough has, or very lately had, a still elder brother living at Sudbury, not less eminent in the arts than the two deceased.

his

A Copy of the Two Incendiary Letters, for the Discovery of the Authors whereof, his Majesty has been pleased to offer his most gracious Pardon to any one of the Accomplices, and Mr. Gainsborough a Reward of 30 l.

London, March the 1st, 1737-8.

M R. Gainsborough, I understand that you have Runed my frind Brock to all Intents and Purposes, which you must Expect to suffer, for Runen a family so Basely as you have done; that is, I mean in the next World you must Expect to suffer for, in this I know your Welth will proteckt you: You have done him so much Dammage, that you can never give him and his family Satisfaction for; for, without Releife, they must Come to the Parrish: So these are to satisfie you, if you Dont Release Brock of the Law Directly, by god you shall never Come to London Safe; for, Dam you, we will have no more Massey than the Devil will have of you; and your Roge of a Lawyer shall, and your Sunn shall, sertainly Drink out of the same Cupp. I do assure you their is a Large Number of Us that will stand by Brock. Your Sunn in Pertickeler, shall never Come to toune safe; for all this troble to Brock, was the Accasion of him; and, God Dam him, the first Site, we will Either shute him or hang him up in Jebbets; Dam the Roge, we was within a Little of his Rogges Ass not a Week ago. Dont flatter your selfe, for unless you Release our friend Brock, if you Bring a troop of men with you to aid you, we will have you from him: Their is 10 or 12 of us that know you all 3; we should have had sume of you before now, if it had not bin for that foole Brock, he put us of on it time after time. If you keep from Coming to toun, we will come Doune and blow you up with Gunpowder. God dam you all, you know the pore fellow profer'd to pay the Roge your Sunn 14 l. when he Come that sad Jorney 1 nigh from your father at London; so I Desire you to send forthwith to Brocks Wife to let her know you will Acquit her husband. *(Turn over)*

Sir, If we had not taken poore Brock in, I do assure you he must a starued. We new him to be an honest lad, so we have taken him in to Ride for us; you know what we Mean; so Release him of the Law directly, or by G—— the furst that is lit of by any of us shall loose his life, so shure as their is a God; but neither you, nor your Lawyer Scabin, I believe, think their is a God; if you did, neither you nor him would strive to Ruin poore familys as you do, and Dam you for rooges, this was no Debt, if it had bin a Debt it had bin an Other Case, so consider what 'tis you have Done and Acquit him; if you don't, by G—— Dam you all, Death shall be your Domes as shure as ever you have Runed this family, and that is sure a nuse. From your oblidged Servants unknown.

Send an Answere to this Directly, to Brocks, or twill be wors for you: I was informed that you could it at your End, that you wold have Brock if he was in England; so Depend upon it, if you Dont acquit him Directly, he shall be shure to give you a Meel that you will not like of: Be shur Dont Come without Being well armed, for Ile assure you we shant; Smuglars seldome go without; so if you have have any Ualue for your Life acquit him at once, as I have said before, for by G—— one or the other shall be Done in a short time; but if you quit Brock Directly, that shant free Scaben, for he have bin a great Roge to an other of our Company, so that we all Resolued, his Roges Carkis shall suffer; for that have Deuour'd hundreds of pore Souls; you have Runed Brocks Mother, for shee was Bound for 70 Pounds for him, and now the Bayles have got shee, and all thorrough your Roges tricks; so Revenge is Sweet.

London, September the 3d, 1738.

M R. Gainsborough, fail not of Quiting Brock Directly of his Troble; if you dont, by G—— Revenged of him your Sun we sertainly will be. I am your friend, to Acquaint you of the Real design; for as shure as ever he was born, he will be put to an Onmersisuest end that can be thought of; he was the Cause of Brocks Troble, and do Assure you, if you dont send to Brocks Wife in a Weeks time, with a free Discharge, our whole Care will be to laye wait for him; tis not his Carring his brace of Pistales that shall frighton us, or Protect him, for they we we dont Ualue. Our Company mett him him upon the Rode sume time ago with his Wife; but we, for the sake of the pore Woman, forbore; but if the above be not granted forthwith, depent on it the next Site, after the tim above is Expired, his Life shall suffer; this is the last Notice that shall Ever be given by Any of our Company; and Sabin, the furst Site, shall drink out of the same cup, for ulcing another of our Company as bad: and if Ever you show or mension this desigt to Any body but your selves, So that tis publish, by G——, by Quiting Brock shant Protect your Sunn; you know you Published the former letter; but take Care you dont do the like now. I am your friend on Known at Present.

Please to observe, the Reason why the above Letters were sent, is, because *Brock* was sued for a just Debt.

The Case is this; *Richard Brock,* of *Margates Inn,* stood indebted to *John Barnard* of *Sudbury,* in the County of *Suffolk,* for Goods sold to him: *Barnard* became a Bankrupt in the Year 1732, and a Commission issued against him at that Time, and Assignees were chosen, to whom the Estate and Effects of the said *Barnard* were Assigned. *Thomas Gainsborough* (to whom the above Letters are sent) being a very large Creditor of *Barnard's,* and living upon the Spot, the said Assignees impowered him to act for them, in getting in the Bankrupt's Debts, and in their Names, to sue such Persons as refused Payment: *Brock* was, for the Space of three Years and upwards, frequently called upon by the said *Thomas Gainsborough* and his Son, for the Payment of the Debt due to *Barnard's* Estate, who as frequently promised, tho' he never did Pay. At length, *Samuel Sabine,* an Attorney at Law, (who is also named in the said Letters) was imployed by the Order of the said Assignees, to sue *Brock* for the Debt, which he accordingly did: *Brock* appeared to the Action, and pleaded the Statute of Limitation, and obliged them to prove the Debt, altho' he made no Defence therein, so that a Verdict passed against him. What he says, of offering to pay Fourteen Pounds to Mr. *Gainsborough's* Son, is intirely false; for he then declared he had no Money; nor would he give any Security for that Sum; and now proposes Payment, by taking away the Lives and Fortunes of those, who only seek to recover a just Debt, by that Law, which is wisely calculated to support Mankind in the Enjoyment of their Rights and Properties.

APPENDIX II:
THE DEATH THREATS

The *London Gazette* published details of the death threats with the offered reward on 26 and 30 September 1738 with the *Daily Gazetteer* publishing the threats themselves the following month on 24 October.

The text appears as it did in 1738 and with modern English spelling:

London, March the 1st, 1737-8
Mr. Gainsborough,

I understand that you have ruined my friend Brock to all Intents and Purposes, which you must expect to suffer, for ruining a family so basely as you have done; that is, I mean in the next World you must expect to suffer for, in this I know your wealth will protect you: You have done so much damage, that you can never give him and his family satisfaction for; for, without release, they must come to the Parish: so these are to satisfy you, if you don't release Brock of the law directly, by God you shall never come to London safe; for, Damn you, we will have no more mercy than the Devil will have of you; and your rouge of a lawyer shall, certainly drink out of the same cup. I do assure you there is a large number of us that will stand by Brock. Your son in particular, shall never come to town safe; for all this trouble to Brock, was the occasion of him; and, God damn him, the first sight, we will either shoot him or hang him up in Gibbets; Damn the rogue, we was within a little of his rogue's arse not a Week ago. Don't flatter yourself, for unless you release our friend Brock, if you bring a troop of men with you to aid you, we will have you from him: Their is 10 or 12 of us that know you all 3; we should have had some of you before now, if it had not been for that fool Brock, he put us on it time after time. If you keep from coming to town, we will come down and blow you up with Gunpowder. God damn you all, you know the poor fellow offered to pay the rogue your son £14 when he came that sad journey one night from your father at London; so I desire you to send forthwith to Brock's wife to let her know you will acquit her husband. (Turn over)

Sir, if we had not taken poor Brock in, I do assure you he would have starved. We knew him to be an honest lad, so we have taken him in to ride for us you know what I mean; so release him of the law directly, or by G— the first that is alighted upon by any of us shall lose his life, so sure as there is a God; but neither you, nor your lawyer Sabine, I believe think there is a God; if you did, neither you nor him would strive to ruin poor families as you do, and damn you for rogues, this was no debt, if it had been a debt it has been another case, so consider what it is you have done and acquit him; if you don't, by G— Damn you all, death shall be you dooms as sure as ever you have ruined this family, and that is sure a noose. From your obliged servants unknown.

Send an answer to this directly to Brocks, or it will be worse for you: I was informed that you could it at your end, that you would have Brock if he was in England; so depend upon it, if you don't acquit him directly, he shall be sure to give you a meal that you will not like: Be sure, don't come without being well armed, for I'll assure you we shan't: Smugglers seldom go without; so if you have any value for your life acquit him at once, as I have said before, for by G— one or the other shall be done in a short time; but if you quit Brock directly that shan't free Sabine, for he have been a great rogue to another of our company, so that we all resolved his rogue's carcass shall suffer; for that have devoured hundreds of poor souls; you have ruined Brock's Mother, for she was bound for 70 pounds for him, and now the bailiffs have got her, and all thorough your rogue's tricks; so Revenge is Sweet.

The Daily Gazetteer.

TUESDAY, OCTOBER 24. 1738. N° 1040.

A Copy of the Two Incendiary Letters, for the Discovery of the Authors whereof, his Majesty has been pleased to offer his most gracious Pardon to any one of the Accomplices, and Mr. Gainsborough a Reward of 30 l.

London, March the 1st, 1737-8.

MR. Gainsborough, I understand that you have Runed my frind Brock to all Intents and Purposes, which you must Expect to suffer, for Runen a family so Basely as you have done; that is, I mean in the next World you must Expect to suffer for, in this I know your Welch will proteck you: You have done him so much Dammage, that you can never give him and his family Satisfaction for; for, without Releise, they must Come to the Parrish: So these to satisfie you, if you Dont Release Brock of the Law Directly, by god you shall never Come to London Safe; for, Dam you, we will have no more Massey than the Devil will have of you; and your Roge of a Lawyer shall, and your Sunn shall, sertainly Drink out of the same Cupp. I do assure you their is a Large Number of Us that will stand by Brock. Your Sunn in Pertickeler, shall never Come to toune safe; for all this troble to Brock, was the Accasion of him; and, God Dam him, the first Site, we will Either shute him or hang him up in Jebbets; Dam the Roge, he was within a Little of his Rogges Ass not a Week ago. Dont flatter your selfe, for unless you Release our friend Brock, if you Bring a troop of men with you to aid you, we will have you from him: Their is 10 or 12 of us that know you all 3; we should have had sume of you before now, if it had not bin for that foole Brock, he put us of on it time after time. If you keep from Coming to toun, we will come Doune and blow you up with Gunpowder. God, dam you all, you know the pore fellow proffer'd to pay the Roge your Sunn 14 l. when he Come that sad Jorney I nigh from your father at London; so, I Desire you to send forthwith to Brocks Wife to let her know you will Acquit her husband. (Turn over)

Sir, If we had not taken poore Brock in, I do assure you he must a starued. We new him to be an honest lad, so we have taken him in to Ride for us; you know what we Mean; so Release him of the Law directly, or by G—— the furst that is lit of by any of us shall loose his life, so shure as their is a God; but neither you, nor your Lawyer Scabin, I believe, think their is a God; if you did, neither you nor him would strive to Ruin poore familys as you do, and Dam you for rooges, this was no Debt, if it had bin a Debt it had bin an Other Case, so consider what 'tis you have Done and Acquit him; if you don't, by G—— Dam you all, Death shall be your Domes as shure as ever you have Runed this family, and that is sure a nufe. From your oblidged Servants unknown.

Send an Answere to this Directly to Brocks, or twill be wors for you: I was informed that you could it at your End, that you wold have Brock if he was in England; so Depend upon it, if you Dont acquit him Directly, he shall be shure to give you a Meel that you will not like of: Be shur Dont Come without Being well armed, for Ile assure you we shant, Smuglars seldome go without; so if you have have any Ualue for your Life acquit him at once, as I have said before, for by G—— one or the other shall be Done in a short time; but if you quit Brock Directly, that shant free Scaben, for he have his a great Roge to an other of our Company, so that we all Resolued his Roges Carkis shall suffer; for that have Devour'd hundreds of pore Souls; you have Runed Brocks Mother, for shee was Bound for 70 Pounds for him, and now the Bayles have got shee, and all thorrough your Roges tricks; so Revenge is Sweet.

London, September the 3d, 1738.

MR. Gainsborough, fail not of Quiting Brock Directly of his Troble; if you dont, by G—— Revenged of him your Sun we sertainly will be. I am your friend, to Acquaint you of the Real design; for as shure as ever he was born, he will be put to an Onmersifuest end that can be thought of; he was the Cause of Brocks Troble, and do Assure you, if you dont send to Brocks Wife in a Weeks time, with a free Discharge, our whole Care will be to laye wait for him; tis not his Carring his brace of Pistales that shall frighton us, or Protect him, for they we we dont Ualue. Our Company mett him him upon the Rode sume time ago with a Wife; but we, for the sake of the pore Woman, forbore; but if the above be not granted forthwith, depent on it the next Site, after the tim above is Expired, his Life shall suffer; this is the last Notice that shall Ever be given by Any of our Company; and Sabin, the furst Site, shall drink out of the same cup, for useing another of our Company as bad: and if Ever you show or mension this desigt to Any body but your selves, So that tis publish, by G——, by Quiting Brock shant Protect your Sunn; you know you Published the former letter; but take Care you dont do the like now. I am your friend on Known at Present.

Please to observe, the Reason why the above Letters were sent, is, because *Brock* was sued for a just Debt.

The Case is this; *Richard Brock*, of *Margates Inn*, stood indebted to *John Barnard* of *Sudbury*, in the County of *Suffolk*, for Goods sold to him: *Barnard* became a Bankrupt in the Year 1732, and a Commission issued against him at that Time, and Assignees were chosen, to whom the Estate and Effects of the said *Barnard* were Assigned. *Thomas Gainsborough* (to whom the above Letters are sent) being a very large Creditor of *Barnard's*, and living upon the Spot, the said Assignees impowered him to act for them, in getting in the Bankrupt's Debts, and in their Names, to sue such Persons as refused Payment: *Brock* was, for the Space of three Years and upwards, frequently called upon by the said *Thomas Gainsborough* and his Son, for the Payment of the Debt due to *Barnard's* Estate, who as frequently promised, tho' he never did Pay. At length, *Samuel Sabine*, an Attorney at Law, (who is also named in the said Letters) was imployed by the Order of the said Assignees, to sue *Brock* for the Debt, which he accordingly did: *Brock* appeared to the Action, and pleaded the Statute of Limitation, and obliged them to prove the Debt, altho' he made no Defence therein, so that a Verdict passed against him. What he says, of offering to pay Fourteen Pounds to Mr. *Gainsborough's* Son, is intirely false; for he then declared he had no Money, nor would he give any Security for that Sum; and now proposes Payment, by taking away the Lives and Fortunes of those, who only seek to recover a just Debt, by that Law, which is wisely calculated to support Mankind in the Enjoyment of their Rights and Properties.

IRELAND.

Castleblaney, Oct. 12. Yesterday being the Anniversary of his Majesty's Coronation, the same was observed here with great Solemnity, and the Right Hon. and Rev. the Lord Blaney gave a handsome Entertainment on the Occasion, where the Healths of his Majesty, the Prince and Princess of Wales, the Duke and the Princesses, were drank; as were those of the Dukes of Devonshire, Dorset and Richmond, &c. There were several Rounds of Guns fired, and Bonfires on every Hill round this Place, and Illuminations almost throughout the whole Town. It is remarkable, that his Lordship's Family have always been zealous in the Protestant Interest, and have shewn, by all Opportunities, their firm Attachment to the illustrious and glorious House of Hanover.

Dublin, Oct. 17. Wednesday last being the Anniversary of his Majesty's Coronation, the Great Guns were fired at the Barracks, and answered by Vollies from the Regiments in Garison; at Noon their Excellencies the Lords Justices met at the Castle, (where a Squadron of Horse attended) and received the Compliments of the Nobility and other Persons of Distinction upon this Occasion; at Night a Play was given by their Excellencies for the Entertainment of the Ladies, when a new Prologue for the Day was spoke by Mr. Griffith, with great Applause; and there were Bonfires, Illuminations, and all other Demonstrations of Joy.

COUNTRY NEWS.

Norwich, Oct. 21. On Tuesday the 10th Instant as Mr. Reynolds, Servant to Mess Attelsey and Aldrich of this City, was riding from Hadiscoe to Yarmouth, he was attacked on Belton Heath by a single Highwayman with a black Wig, black Complexion, a black Beard of 9 or 10 Days Growth, a bluish Riding Coat, and mounted on a Red Roan scrubby Horse, with a rough Mane and Coat: He said to Mr. Reynolds, Damn you, have I staid for you all this Morning? Unmount, or I will shoot you this Minute: Upon which Mr. Reynolds asked him, what he would have? He replied, I will have your Mare and your Bags; and upon that fired a Pistol at him, the Ball of which he heard whiz into the Furrs; whereupon Mr. Reynolds clapt Spurs to his Mare, and rode off as fast as he could; but the Highwayman rode after him, and fired a second Pistol at him, the Bullet of which grazed on the Sleeve of his Great Coat; but being better mounted than the Highwayman, he outrode him, and got clear off: The Highwayman, he saw, had more Pistols in a Belt under his Great Coat; and after he left pursuing him, he rode away towards Somerly: This is the Truth of the Fact, as sworne before Justice Milles of Yarmouth.

On Tuesday last a Man was robbed in Harpham-Lane, between Larlingford and Attleborough, by two Highwaymen, as he was coming to Norwich; they took from him Four Guineas and a Shilling, but returned him the Shilling to bear his Charges to Norwich.

FOREIGN PORTS.

Elsineur, Oct. 18. N. S. My last was of the 14th, since the following Masters have arrived, viz. On the 14th, George Joad, from Dantzick for London: On the 15th, John Moody, for Hull; Roger Curling, and Samuel Stephens, for London; Nathaniel Alloway, for Bristol, all four from Petersburg; Robert Craig, from Riga for Waterford: On the 16th, Thomas Harvey, from Petersburg for Newcastle; Thomas Spencer, and John Dowson, from Petersburg; Thomas Story, from Narva; Ambrose Partis, and John Dear, from Stockholm; William Curtis, from Riga, all 6 for London: On the 18th, Robert Wallis, from Stockholm for Portsmouth; Christopher Soller, from Copenhagen for ——; Charles Lowndes, from Petersburg for Liverpool.

'The outward bound are sailed, with the Wind 'at S. E. which continues with rainy, blowing and 'unconstant Weather.

Elsineur, Oct. 21. N. S. My last was of the 18th Instant, since the following Masters have arrived, viz. On the 19th, Cornelius Barrett, from Newcastle for Koningsburg: On the 21st, Peter Sheppard, from Petersburg for Bristol; John Ritchie, Jun. from Leith for Dantzick.

'Those bound for the Baltick are sailed, with the 'Wind at N. W. which continues, whereby the 'Captains Lowndes and Sheppard, are detained in 'this Road.

HOME PORTS.

Whitehaven, Oct. 18. Arrived the Argyle, Brownrigg, from Virginia.

Newcastle, Oct. 20. Arrived the Newcastle Merchant, Harvey, from Petersburg.

Liverpool, Oct. 20. Arrived the Hamilton, Ireland, from Virginia.

Falmouth, Oct. 19. Since my last arrived the Townshend Packet, Cooper, from the Groyne. Sailed the Expedition Packet, Clies, for Lisbon. Yesterday came in the St. Peter, Lamport; the Theophila, Goddard; the Fame, Harris, to load Fish for the Streights; the Endeavour, Bradford, for Seville. Wind W.

Dartmouth, Oct. 20. The 17th at Night, came in and remains, the Marquis, Gardner, of and from London for Cadiz: On the 18th, the Hopewell, Ferguson, of and from Dunbar, and sailed again Yesterday for Barcelona. Arrived Yesterday, and this Day, the Endeavour, Land, for London; and the Emanuel and Sarah, Lawrence, both of this Place from Newfoundland. Wind blows hard at S. S. W.

Southampton.

London, September 3rd, 1738

Mr. Gainsborough,

Fail not of quitting Brock directly of his trouble; if you don't, by G— revenged of him your son we certainly will be. I am your friend, to acquaint you of the Real design, for as sure as ever he was born, he will be put to such an ominous end that can be thought of; he was the cause of Brock's trouble, and do assure you, if you don't send to Brock's wife in a Weeks time, with a free Discharge, our whole care will be to lay wait for him, carrying his pair of pistols that shall not frighten us, nor protect him, for them we don't value. Our company met him upon the road some time ago with his wife; but we, for the sake of the poor woman held off; but if the above not be granted forthwith, depend on it the next sight, after the time above is expired, his life shall suffer; this is the last Notice that shall Ever be given by any of our company; and Sabine, the first sight, shall drink of the same cup, for using another of our company as bad: and if ever you show or mention this design to anybody but yourselves, so that it is published, by G—, by quitting Brock shan't protect your son; you know you published the former letter; but take care you don't do the like now. I am your friend unknown at Present.

Please to observe, the Reason why the above Letters were sent, is, because Brock was sued for a just Debt.

The Case is this: Richard Brock, of Margates Inn, stood indebted to John Barnard of Sudbury, in the County of Suffolk, for goods sold to him: Barnard became a bankrupt in the year 1732, and a commission issued against him at that time, and assignees were chosen, to whom the estate and effects of the said Barnard were assigned. Thomas Gainsborough (to whom the Letters were sent) being a very large creditor of Barnard's, and living upon the spot, the said assignees empowered him to act for them, in getting in the bankrupt's debts, and in their names to sue such persons as refused payment: Brock was, for the space of three years and upwards, frequently called upon by the said Thomas Gainsborough and his son, for the payment of the debt due to Barnard's estate, who as frequently promised, though he never did pay. At length, Samuel Sabin, an Attorney at Law, (who is also in the said letters) was employed by the order of the said assignees, to sue Brock for the debt, which he accordingly did: Brock appeared to the action, and pleaded the Statute of Limitation, and obliged them to prove the debt, although he made no defence therein, so that a verdict passed against him. What he says, of offering to pay Fourteen Pounds to Mr. Gainsborough's son, is entirely false; for he then declared he had no money, nor would he give any security for that sum: and now proposes payment, by taking away the lives and fortunes of those, who only seek to recover a just debt, by that law, which is wisely calculated to support mankind in the enjoyment of their rights and properties.

GAINSBOROUGH'S HOUSE WOULD LIKE TO THANK EVERYONE FOR THEIR SUPPORT

Benefactors

The Heritage Lottery Fund
Timothy and Mary Clode
The George John & Sheilah
Livanos Charitable Trust
The Linbury Trust
Babergh District Council
Garfield Weston Foundation
New Anglia LEP
Foyle Foundation
The Wolfson Foundation
The John Ellerman Foundation
David Pike
The Band Trust
The Lord Belstead Charitable
Settlement
J Paul Getty Jnr Charitable Trust
The Pilgrim Trust
The Finnis Scott Foundation
Maggi Hambling CBE
Lowell Libson
Andrew Lloyd-Webber
Foundation
John Beale
Esmée Fairbairn Foundation
The Paul Mellon Centre for
Studies in British Art
Suffolk County Council
Sudbury Town Council
Vanners Silk Weavers
Anthony Wheeler Bequest

Donors

de Laszlo Foundation
Sir Siegmund Warburg's Voluntary
Settlement
Rogers, Stirk, Harbour & Partners
Charitable Foundation
John Gambart Webb Bequest
James Hughes-Hallett
AIM Association of Independent
Museums
The Arts Society
Ernest Cook Trust
Babara Whatmore Charitable
Trust

Robert Davey
John Osborn
Richard Mansell-Jones
Sir John Hoskyns Charitable Trust
The Doric Charitable Trust
Lowell Libson
Coral Samuel Charitable Trust
Phillips Fund
Sir Edward Lewis Foundation
Stanley Foundation
Surrey Square Charitable Trust
David Tyler
The Scarfe Charitable Trust
Lord and Lady Marlesford
John Laing Charitable Trust
Aurelius Charitable Trust
The Henry Moore Foundation
Association for Suffolk Museums
Brocklebank Charitable Trust
The Constable Trust
The Radcliffe Trust
Wallace Charity Trust
Alfred Williams Charitable Trust
Art Fund Suffolk Branch
Faith Robinson
John Sheeran
P & S Schafler
Heathgate Charitable Trust
Timothy Colman Charitable Trust
Chivers Trust
Basil Slaughter Trust
The Schorr Collection
Nicholas Antill
Dedham Vale ANOB
Colchester Borough Council
Bevan Charitable Trust
Contemporary Art Auction -
Artists
The Silk Manufacturers of
Sudbury
Reeman Dansie
Jonathan Lambert Fine Jewellery
The Swan at Long Melford
Nethergate Brewery Co Ltd
The Trustees of Gainsborough's
House

Mulberry Patrons

Lord Abinger
Nicholas & Jenny Antill
Martin & Jane Bailey
Simon & Melanie Barrett
Marcia Brocklebank
David & Mary Burr
Christie's
Timothy & Mary Clode
Robert Erith
Lady Clare Euston
Nigel & Chris Evans
Rupert & Robin Hambro
Mark Harris
Faith Hines
Lowell & Rowena Libson
Tim Llewellyn OBE
Suzanne Marriott
Brian & Valerie Moody
David & Alison Moore-Gwyn
Philip Mould OBE
John Osborn
Penny Payne
David Pike
Louise Pollock
Nella & Geoffrey Probert
Griff Rhys Jones
Ann E Smith
Lord & Lady Stevenson
Christopher Stewart-Smith
Alan Swerdlow and Jeremy
Greenwood
Heather Tilbury Phillips
Nicholas & Jane Turner
Paul & Vanessa Watchman
Wilf Weeks OBE & Annie Weeks

THANK YOU TO OUR
MULBERRY PATRONS,
PATRONS, FRIENDS AND ALL
OUR VOLUNTEERS